San Marco: Celebrating 90 Years

- George Foote & Robin Robinson

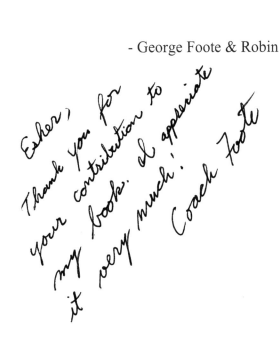

Esher,

Thank you for your contribution to my book. I appreciate it very much!

Coach Foote

Silent E Publishing Company

Silent E Publishing Company
4446 Hendricks Ave, #141
Jacksonville, Florida, USA
All Rights Reserved

ISBN-13 978-1-941091-07-4

First Print / First Edition

10 9 8 7 6 5 4 3 2 1

For Cassius

Table of Contents

Introduction
George Foote

Depending on how you look at it, 90 years is an eternity or a blink of an eye. But regardless of the perspective, I see marking San Marco's 90 years as a great opportunity to celebrate and reflect.

The fabric of our community has many threads and a list includes things like Little League sports, award winning schools, churches that reach out and become part of the community, civic groups that help guide and preserve, scout troops, musicians, museums, libraries, and businesses where the proprietors know your name. My list of neighbors and friends is long and in almost every case these are people who genuinely care about each other and our community. We have a healthy dose of civic pride in San Marco and the many hands make light labor axiom applies in most cases.

Our goal with this book is threefold. First, Robin, one of our foremost resident historians, takes us on a journey *Through the Decades.* Starting with Telfair Stockton's idea for an Italian themed development, continuing through time to recount the evolution of San Marco's many local businesses and finally, wrapping up by illuminating the growth and preservation efforts in the later decades. After that, we give voice to members of the community to reflect on their own San Marco experiences in the chapter titled "90 *Voices from San Marco.*" In some cases we have accounts of childhood experiences and others talk about events, organizations, and traditions. In total, it's a snapshot of life in San Marco and we are grateful for those that were able to contribute to this section of the book. Finally, we have fashioned our own version of a time capsule with some documentation of accomplishments in San Marco which includes everything from Garden Circle presidents, to Eagle Scouts, to attendees of the *"Feast of Carnevale,"* a party to celebrate San Marco's 90 years.

Assessing San Marco as a place, gives me thoughts of my friends of many years, Terri and Larry Haber. The Habers were the first ever residents of the Disney designed community, Celebration, Florida. Celebration was named the "New Community of the Year" in 2001 by the Urban Land Institute and touted as a walkable, environmentally friendly mixed use development that included homes, apartments, a shopping district, office buildings, schools, movie theater & churches. It was a big deal at the time and described by some as an important part of the neo-urbanism movement. After visiting the Habers for the first time and touring Celebration, I agreed that it was a fantastic place, but I couldn't help but think of San Marco and how we have all of these wonderful things in our community and much more. In the chapters that follow, I think Robin and I, and the many contributors to this effort, will provide supporting evidence for this.

To get us started, one of my favorite stories from the neighborhood comes from my good friend Jeff Trippe and the topic, near to my heart, is Hendricks Avenue Baptist (HAB) baseball. All three of my children played baseball there and I spent 17 years there as a coach. I made a large group of friends and built up a lifetime of great memories at those ballparks. Jeff's story is a small and somewhat comical glimpse from that corner of the community.

It Happened One Spring – Eventually.

Sadly, I know that as I sit here at my preferred café table, the old baseball fields on Hendricks Avenue are lying brown and fallow, as "winter" in Jacksonville grinds on. Yet we all might take comfort in knowing that soon enough, the old reliable tractor will sputter to life once again, hungry for grass seed and freshly turned dirt. Back in the day, Tom Morris, the perennial commissioner of the youth baseball program of the Hendricks Avenue Community Athletic Association, who has served in that role for about as long as Franco ruled Spain, will put on his walking shorts, pull his socks up to his knees, and confidently resume command of home plate, and try-outs will ensue yet again at one of the city's oldest and most honored parks. Let the Red Sox and Yankees make their mega-deals, leave the Roger Clemenses of the world to wrestle with their demons...THIS is what baseball in America is really about.

Once upon a time, the league was known as H.A.B. – Hendricks Avenue Baptist, after the church which owns the grounds. When I coached there from 1993 till 2003, it was a humble venue. Generally, our teams were made up of wholesome kids from nice homes, with a few good ballplayers sprinkled amongst each division of six or eight teams, but our all-star teams could never really compete with those from the bigger programs around town. The majority of our players were very pleasant boys and girls who tried very hard in just about everything they did, but there were no future pros among them. We liked to call them "scrappy."

My friend George and I coached together for all of those seasons, and our sons grew up together on those fields. I was a good deal thinner then, and was a devil with a fungo bat, and George taught sportsmanship with great skill: "No, Doug, I do not want you to throw at the heads of the other team's hitters. This is only little league after all. And no, Tommy, you may not moon the opposing team's fans from right field. Why not? Because no one wants to see that, that's why not." In general, I think we had a positive influence.

There was this one kid, however: Shane. Shane took a particular approach to the craft of baseball, in that he chose the path of independence in all situations. Signals when he came up to bat? Pointless. Attempting to position him when he was in the outfield? You might as well be shouting into a gale. Shane had his own way of playing the game. He even eschewed our collection of high-tech aluminum bats in favor of an ancient wood fungo bat given him by his grandfather, which was as long as Shane was tall. I felt certain that if he ever did accidentally make contact with the ball on one of his from-the-heels swings, that bat would splinter into a thousand pieces and probably maim some bystander.

George and I always liked to ensure that every kid got a game ball at some point during the season for doing something well – getting a key hit, making a good play in the field – but sometimes it was a bit of a stretch ("And today's game ball goes to Joey, who did a great job running the bases today.") Still, it was worth it to see the face of some kid, who might never have received any sort of special recognition before, light up with pride.

Well, we struggled for weeks to come up with a reason to award a game ball to Shane. One Saturday we nearly gave it to him for vaulting gazelle-like over the waist-high left field fence after a home run ball which the opponent's clean-up hitter had just emphatically swatted for a grand slam. The irony in this was that ordinarily we couldn't even get him to jog out to his position. Still, it was an extraordinary effort, if unnecessary. But we held off, hoping we would be able to reward Shane for some feat which did not involve the other team scoring on us.

Finally, it came down to the last game of the season, and Shane had still not received a game ball. George and I paced the dugout anxiously when our team was in the field. Then, in the third inning, Shane was hit by a pitch in the left arm. When the side was retired, George grinned and slapped me on the back. "There it is, Coach!" he said gleefully. "Seems that Shane has 'taken one for the team' and earned his game ball."

"Do you really think we should give him the ball for getting hit by a pitch?" I asked. "I mean, he didn't even try to get out of the way. Frankly, I don't think he even knew he'd been hit until the umpire told him."

George frowned. "Hmm. Maybe you're right. But we're down to the wire here. We've got to give it to him. Don't we?"

I shrugged.

Fortunately, we were relieved of our terrible burden in the game's last inning, when Shane came to bat again. In fact, it was the very last at-bat of the entire season, and he was the very last batter. The contest was tied, 4-4, and Shane coolly tapped the clay from his shoes with his antique thunder-stick. He stepped into the box, apparently undaunted by having been plugged his last time up, or else simply lacking any recollection of it. Then, on the first pitch, a fastball right down the middle, he reared back and swung as if the fate of the free world depended on it. Miraculously, wood met horsehide with a solid smack, and the ball rose, sailing up, up, over the center field fence and far beyond it, landing in the sparse grass and trickling toward the mucky woods behind the gas station which fronted Hendricks Avenue. It was his only hit all season – a walk-off home run to win our last game.

I looked over at George. He was gazing off into the distance where the ball gone, like a man trying to resolve one of the universe's great riddles. Then he looked over at me, mouth open as if to speak, but no sound emanated.

"Pretty good," I said.

"Nice swing," George said.

Afterward, Shane accepted his game ball humbly, wordlessly, but with an air of propriety, as if all of this had been ordained somehow, by divine intervention. And perhaps it had. Who were we to say?

-Jeff Trippe (2003)

Through the Decades
90 Years in San Marco
Robin Robinson

THE BIRTH OF SAN MARCO - 1926

South Jacksonville was a small town located on the southbank of the St. Johns River in the early 20th century. The river was alive with boat traffic delivering people from one side of the river to the other, but it wasn't until construction of the first automobile/pedestrian bridge to span the river that easy access to the southbank became a reality. The St. Johns River Bridge was opened on July 1, 1921 and made the area in South Jacksonville ripe for development.

Fresh from his successful development of Avondale, an upscale subdivision across the river, Telfair Stockton set his sights on South Jacksonville. In 1925 he platted the subdivision which he named San Marco along with the business center of San Marco. In 1926 the first building was completed in San Marco Square. The first business located in it was the Town Pump Drugs and Sundries. It remains the anchor of the Square today as the San Marco Building, notable with its Mediterranean style and designated a National Historic Landmark.

Stockton's inspiration for his new development was inspired by the Piazza di San Marco in Venice, Italy. He changed the names of the streets to conform with his Italian theme. Forrest Avenue became San Marco Boulevard and the river road was renamed Rialto Place. The center of the square featured a tiered fountain which was later topped with a wrought iron finial. One of the first businesses in the square was the Gulf Gas station. Both these landmarks were located on the triangle of land which today is Balis Park.

Within a stone's throw from the Square, Landon Junior/Senior High School was erected in 1927 on site of Julia Landon's childhood home. She sold the property to the Duval County Board of Public Instruction in 1925. The school was named after her in recognition of her lifelong devotion to the education of Southside's children.

THE GROWTH OF SAN MARCO SQUARE - 1930's

Setzer's Grocery completed its store in the square in 1937. It boasted 100,000 square feet of space, making it one of the largest grocery stores in the South. People from Arlington as well as those on the Southside shopped at the store. Other businesses in San Marco Square at that time were Sam's Liquors, The Economy Dry Cleaners and Dyers, Goode's Bakery, the Landon five-cents-to-a-dollar store, the San Marco Market, the San Marco Pharmacy and the Dixie Cleaners.

The Little Theatre in San Marco Square was also built in 1937 by Whatley, Davin & Company. Its construction was made possible through fundraising efforts and the generous donation of local resident, Carl S. Swisher of the Jno H. Swisher & Son Tobacco Company. The theatre is listed on the National Register of Historic Places and holds the distinction of being the oldest continually operating community theater group in the country.

The following year in 1938 the San Marco Theatre opened for business in its Art Deco building The location of

14

such a theatre in San Marco was viewed at the time as a tangible expression of confidence in the future growth and importance of the San Marco neighborhood. Its opening festivities included Mayor George Blume purchasing the first ticket (for 25 cents) and the former Mayor John Alsop assisting in the operation of the modern picture equipment to show the first film.

In 1939 Herman Jackson Dry Cleaning was one of the first businesses to be established in the north side of the square. For years it was the "go-to" place for the cleaning and preservation of wedding gowns. The business has moved into a different location, but is still has a presence in the Square today.

SAN MARCO SQUARE - 1940's

The South Jacksonville Baptist Church moved from its Kipp Street location to San Marco Square in 1940, changing its name to Southside Baptist Church. Its location at the corner of Atlantic and Hendricks gave it room to grow into its present day complex of buildings.

Station 13 of the Jacksonville Fire Department was built in the San Marco Square and placed into service in 1941.

One of the sights in San Marco Square in the 1940's which seems strange to us today was the dominating presence of huge lighted billboards above some of the storefronts.

Businesses in the Square in the 1940's were Setzer's Grocery Store, Marsh Kornegay Photography, Ferrell Bros. Jewelers, San Jose Beauty Center, Sam's Liquor, Duval

15

Laundry, Rosier's Barber and Beauty Shop, Jack's Delicatessen, Stewart's Five Cent to One Dollar Store, The Stag Shop (men's store), Miller Electric Company, Arthur Williams Drug Store, Ladd Bros. Children's Wear, Utsey & Lester Shoes, The Town Pump, San Marco Bakery, Herman Jackson Cleaners, Arrow-Zoric Cleaners, Lovett's Food Store, Carleton Drug, San Marco Theatre, Gulf Oil Filling Station, S. H. Kress, Reynolds Piano Company, Lane Drug Store, Bowling Center of South Jacksonville, the Little Theatre, and Southern Bell Telephone & Telegraph Company.

LOCAL LIFE - 1950's

In the 1950's San Marco's entertainment highlights that residents remember from their childhood were the San Marco Theatre and the Southside Bowling Center. Children would walk to the square with their coins and go watch a movie, perhaps a double feature, and go bowling where the pin boys in the back would reset the pins for you. Both establishments were air conditioned which was a real treat in the sweltering summer.

In 1954 the interstate highway system was constructed through Southside with the completion of the Fuller Warren Bridge. The expressway demolished most of the early business and residential areas of the former City of South Jacksonville. Businesses and churches moved south nearer the Square.

Businesses in the Square during that decade included: Marsh Kornegay Photographer, Ferrell Jewelers, San Jose Beauty Center, Sam's Liquor Store, Duval Laundry, Rosier's Barber Shop, Jack's Delicatessen, Stewart's Five Cent to One Dollar Store, The Stag Shop, Dixon Electric, Williams Drug

Store, Ladd Bros. Children's Shop, Town Pump, San Marco Bakery, Herman Jackson Cleaners, Arrow-Zoric Cleaners, Lovett's Food Store, Carlton Drugs, Tony's Head to Foot Shop, Tony's Grill, San Marco Theatre, Gulf Oil Filling Station, S. H Kress, Bowling Center of South Jacksonville, Lane Drug Store, Little Theatre, and Southern Bell Telephone.

1960's

The San Marco Merchants Association was formed in 1964. It has operated since then to coordinate projects and events in the Square and has been a close partner with San Marco Preservation Society. SMMA's Holiday Magic event in early December each year is a tradition that is dear to the hearts of San Marco residents.

More clothing stores made an appearance in the square in the 60's meaning better all-around shopping.

Businesses in the 60's included: Stokes Auto Service, Food Fair Grocers, Dino Distributors Auto Shop, San Marco Hair Styles, San Jose Beauty Center, Rosier's Barber Shop, Dixie Cleaners, San Marco Vogue Shop, Stand 'N Snack, Jeri's Liquors, Southern Appliances, American Import Lighting, Giles San Marco Pharmacy, Jones Apothecary, Jill Stevens Bridal Salon, Duval Real Estate, Town Pump Tavern, Mim's San Marco Bakery, McDonald Stamp Co., Herman Jackson Cleaners, Freddie's House of Yarn, Larry's Shoe Store, Williams Casual Shop, Lowe's Drugs, White's of San Marco, San Marco Theatre, Gulf Service Station, Peterson's 5 & 10, Utsey's Shoe Store, Coley-Walker Drug Store, Arcade Men's Shop, The Silk Shop, Underwood Jewelers, Nancy Scott Women's Clothes, Marsh Kornegay Photographer, Polly's San

Marco Stylists, Little Theatre, Southern Bell Telephone & Telegraph, Jan's of Jacksonville, Ben Jones Interior Design, and Sibyl's Hair Stylist.

AGING OF THE SQUARE - 1970's

In 1975, local residents and businessmen came together to address the aging of San Marco Square and, more specifically, the aging fountain in the square. They wanted to take a proactive approach to tackle the problems which led to the formation of the San Marco Preservation Society (SMPS). Thus began its first attempts to fix the fountain and to begin formulating a long range plan to revitalize the square. SMPS has remained strong throughout the years working to tighten zoning laws, sponsor beautification projects and work with the City to renovate its streets and amenities including the construction and expansion of Balis Park.

By the 1970's grocery stores had disappeared from the Square. Setzer's Grocery Store, established in the 1930's, and eventually sold out to Food Fair. Subsequently, Benjamin Setzer focused on his other up and coming business known as Pic 'N Save. He opened the business up in the same space Setzer's Grocery Store had previously occupied at 1950 San Marco Boulevard. It was a store well liked in San Marco Square and residents remember fondly that you could buy anything from a gallon of paint to a loaf of bread in the store. It was the all-around place for all your needs in pre-Walmart days.

Some businesses which were located in the square in the 1970's were: Stokes Auto Service, Pic 'N Save, Esquire Formal Wear, San Marco Hair Styles, San Jose Beauty Shop,

Mr. Sandwich, Dixie Cleaners, Bold City Hearing Aid, Stand 'N Snack, Jill Stevens Bridal Shop, Emporium of Jacksonville, American Import Lighting, Bath and Linen Shoppe, Jones Apothecary, Rosier Barber Shop, Town Pump Tavern, Mim's San Marco Bakery, Herman Jackson Cleaners, Merle Norman Cosmetics, Larry's Shoe Store, Abe Livert Records, Health Nut House, White's of San Marco, San Marco Theatre, Gulf Service Station, Peterson's 5 & 10, Utsey's Shoes, Coley-Walker Drug Store, Arcade Men's Shop, The Silk Shop, Underwood Jewelers, Purcell Women's Clothes, San Marco Bookstore, Marsh Kornegay Photographer, General Office Furniture and Supply, Paraphernalia Tresses Stylist, Theatre Jacksonville, Southern Bell T & T, Yana of Greece, and Harvey Kirby Auto Service.

REBIRTH OF THE SQUARE - 1980's

In 1983 the San Marco Square Master Plan was completed. Its design delineated plans to revitalize the Square in a series of phases. Planting trees was among the first order of business as well as negotiations to purchase the empty dirt lot in the middle of the square where the Gulf Service Station was previously located. Councilman Gifford Grange's success in purchasing the property for the City laid the groundwork for turning the property into a beautiful park. Once the property was purchased local architect, Andy Liliskis, designed the layout for the park's fountain, gazebo and flowering trees. Alba Balis made a donation to bring the plan to fruition in memory of her late husband, Sheffield Balis.

In June 1987 the groundbreaking took place for Balis Park and in February 1988 Balis Park was dedicated under the direction of Councilwoman Ginny Myrick. The park was made possible through the generous Balis donation and a joint partnership between SMPS, SMMA and the City of Jacksonville. A special thanks went to Skip Alcorn and Debbie White for their work on the project.

In 1980 The Wardroom, Ltd., opened in the Square and has remained a pillar of the Square ever since. It boasts a wide array of home decor and gift selections.

In 1981 The Loop opened its first restaurant in San Marco Square. Mike and Terry Schneider chose to open and an upscale, but casual, restaurant with high quality food served quickly for families on the go. San Marco residents readily took to The Loop and it has grown to a number of locations in North Carolina and Florida.

In 1983 local resident Phyllis Lockwood opened her new business which she named Peterbrooke Chocolatier. Her mission was to bring the art of European chocolate making to the United States, offering a wide selection of European styled handmade chocolates. Her flagship store was wildly successful and Peterbrooke now has locations throughout the Southeast.

Businesses located in the square in the 1980's included: Paul Lewis Tire, Pic 'N Save, Impressions, San Marco Hairstyles, Nail Sculpting by Roxanne, Edwards Pipe & Tobacco, Dixie Cleaners, Bookends Paperback Exchange, Stand 'N Snack, Maxine's Stout Shop, Emporium of Jacksonville, Geisenhof Gifts, The Write Touch, Ward Lariscy Interior Design, Pampered Chef, San Marco Bookstore, Peterbrooke Chocolatier, St. Marks Restaurant, Cafe on the Square, Out to Lunch sandwich shop, Herman Jackson Cleaners, J. D. Brown Antiques & Oriental Rugs, White's of San Marco, San Marco Theatre, Peterson's 5 & 10, Utsey's

Shoes, Barnett Bank, Arcade Men's Shop, The Loop, Underwood Jewelers, Reynolds Art Gallery, The Silk Store, Paraphernalia Tresses, Little Theatre, Southern Bell T & T, Health Nut House, J. D. Howell men's store, Barefoot in the Park shoes, and Harvey Kirby's Auto Service.

FURTHER STRIDES - 1990's

After the community struggled with repairing and decoratively painting the 50+ year old fountain without satisfactory results, Zim Boulos issued a challenge to redesign the fountain by announcing a contest co-sponsored by the American Institute of Architects in 1992. Utilizing the lion symbol of St. Mark, the winning design by Alan Wilson and Angela Schifanella featured three lions in different poses. Hugh Nicholson of Tallahassee was chosen as the sculptor. With a great deal of effort put into fundraising, the new fountain became a reality and was unveiled at the Carnevale di San Marco on April 18, 1997 to the awe and praise of all present at the celebration. The Three Lions Fountain has become the signature image for San Marco, one which we proudly display.

In 1991 the San Marco Garden Circle installed a "Welcome to Historic San Marco" sign at the intersection of Atlantic Boulevard and Kings Road. Included in the makeover of the small park were gaslights, landscaping and an historical plaque. Martha Stewart of national renown was present at the dedication of the renovated park.

Early in the 1990's the San Marco Garden Circle, as a gift to the community, put up a Christmas tree in the gazebo in

21

Balis Park. They have continued to do so every year and is the focal point of the square during the holidays.

Sadly, Pic 'N Save filed bankruptcy and closed its doors in 1994. It left a gaping hole in the Square which has since been divided up for the establishment of several other businesses.

Businesses in the square in the 1990's include: Paul Lewis Tire, Impressions, Mickler's Landing Inc., Bound & Cave leather shop, Dependable Cleaners, Smooth Ventures Inc., San Marco Deli, Custom Rug Gallery, The Write Touch, Wardroom, Ltd., Richard's Village Nursery, Mimi's Kitchen Shop & Cooking School, San Marco Bookstore, Cafe on the Square, Herman Jackson Cleaners, Cafe Carmon, White's of San Marco, San Marco Theatre, Chelsea Photographic, Alder Interior Design, Barnett Bank, The Grotto, The Loop, Edwards Pipe & Tobacco, Krista Eberle's women's shop, Peterbrooke Chocolatier, Theatre Jacksonville, Underwood Jewelers, Bath & Linen Shoppe, and Starling's Produce.

EFFORTS CONTINUE INTO THE 2000's

The early part of this decade was highlighted by the addition of a number of amazing sculptures in the Square. Beginning with the installation of the Three Lions Fountain in 1997, other sculptures were added including "Windy Days" (affectionately known locally as the "Kite Kids"), the "Entertainer" and the "Journey of Imagination." Private donors were most generous in the support of these installations.

In 2008 Fire Station 13 was renovated. Many donors contributed to the project, but the firemen themselves did all the work including painting the exterior and interior, implementing a new floor plan, refinishing floors, landscaping and laying pavers. The results were shown to the public during the 2008 SMPS Home Tour.

In 2012 work began on changing the streetscape in the Square to eliminate the stoplight on Atlantic Boulevard. The resulting solution for managing traffic freed up green space with which to greatly expand Balis Park. SMMA and SMPS worked together to raise the funds for the park improvements. Doug Skiles provided the design and spearheaded the project. The greatly expanded Balis Park opened with fanfare in the fall of 2013.

Businesses in the square during this time included: 5 Sisters Boutique, Definition Fitness, Firehouse Subs, In the Kitchen, Sushi Rock Cafe, Three Lions Antiques, Impressions, Miriam's Jeweler's Pizza Palace, Rosie True women's shop, Smoothie King, Dependable Cleaners, San Marco Deli, The Write Touch, San Marco Bookstore, Duck Duck Goose children's shop, Pom's Thai Bistro, Square One, Starbucks, Herman Jackson Cleaners, Leila's, Mimi's, Cafe Carmon, Luna, Karl's Clothiers, Pick of the Crop, San Marco theatre, San Marco Petites, Moe's Southwest Grill, Adler Interior Design, Bank of America, The Grotto, The Loop, B. Langston Antiques, Gallery Framery, Edward's Pipe & Tobacco, Krista Eberle, Monograms & More, Theatre Jacksonville, Underwood Jewelers, Bath & Linen Shoppe, and Mathew's Market.

90 Voices from San Marco
Collected Essays

Skip Alcorn – San Marco - the 80's - a decade of transition

When we moved to San Marco in 1979, we bought a house at 833 Sorrento Rd, having looked at it with a structural engineer with the possibility that it may need to be torn down. But the 1920's vintage lady had great bones, so we made the plunge for $70,000 and would spend the next 20 years putting life back into the beautiful lady she once was.

San Marco itself was a bit run down. Most homeowners were either first or second generation from the 20's and 30's, so many homes were a bit "overgrown" with planting There weren't many kids to play with our 4 and 7 year old daughters, but we saw the potential of this grand old neighborhood. A few houses had started the revitalization, and there just seemed to be a great neighborhood waiting to happen.

San Marco Square was a bit old as well. The legendary Town Pump was a favorite watering hole for many of the older generations living nearby. Mims Bakery was the vintage bakery and lunch bar where you felt young going in. But great stuff. Pic-N-Save anchored the north end of the block, where you could always get your last second groceries and meds within easy walking distance. And in the middle of the Square (where Balis Park now resides) sat the centerpiece, the Gulf service station, owned by an always hospitable Carl West. White's Book Store and many other small shops circled the decaying "wedding cake" fountain, which had a history of its own from many attempts to "put lipstick on a pig."

My wife, Peggy, first got involved with a small but active organization called San Marco Preservation Society. Several dozen people were pushing through a rather ambitious agenda to revitalize San Marco Square. Led by two neighborhood dwelling architects with Kemp Bunch and Jackson (now KBJ), Jim Rink and Tom Reynolds, a revitalization plan had been initiated by them, turning to a University of Florida grad student in landscape architecture, Andy Lilliskas. This revitalization plan would be his graduate thesis. When we got involved, it had been beautifully completed, and the basis from which SMPS would direct its efforts towards a new San Marco Square.

The plan was submitted to the city, and just happened to coincide with a citywide long term storm water drainage initiative. This involved quite a bit of street demolition, new 48" storm pipes, and street resurfacing. Certain members of SMPS started meeting with the city and its engineer of record to coordinate our design into theirs. We were concerned about the devastation with the Hemming Plaza revitalization and what it did to shop owners there. Meanwhile, a private shop owner initiative of its own was happening our square.

John Currington and Keith Kimball had just finished purchasing the half block from the theatre to the old Town Pump building. Extensive renovations had begun to the theatre and the centerpiece restaurant in the middle of the block, White's Bookstore had also done extensive renovations. On further investigation, we saw the street and sidewalk demolition at Hemming Plaza downtown and saw much the same intended for San Marco. This probably began the greatest "rallying cries" to ever happen in San Marco.

Another significant thing happened in the early 80's. Our Gulf service station owner, Carl West, was murdered in north Jacksonville. As we mourned the loss of a true friend and neighbor, the station ceased to be open. While being iconic with its numerous upgrades from the early 1900's, suddenly the station lay idle. We met with Councilman Gifford Grange about some of his discretionary funds that he could use for his district, and were able to purchase the station for $110,000. The site fit into the master plan drawn both by Lilliskas and the engineers hired by the city.

Meanwhile the San Marco Merchants Association was gaining steam. Debbie White (now Debbie Fewell) with White's Bookstore and Judy Blumberg with Bounds Cave put together spectacular Holiday magic events in the square. The coinciding San Marco Home Tour also went to another level with spectacular renovated homes and incredible volunteer efforts. The neighborhood lit up for the Holidays. The first live manger scene was initiated on the corner of Hendricks Ave and Largo Rd, a legacy to this day.

As city plans evolved in the mid 80's, we finally were able to see final plans and specs. Much like Hemming Plaza, we determined that most of the streets and sidewalks were coming up in mass. Likewise, the underground drainage would extend down Largo Rd behind the square, and in the process, cause most of the massive live oaks to be removed. Yet most people were unaware of all of this. So "town hall' meetings were called at The Little Theatre to bring awareness to what might happen.

The city put the Square revitalization out for bid, and the low bid came back at $2.5 million. This was within the budget the city had figured. Meanwhile SMPS decided it

27

needed bigger political clout to foster better relationships with city officials. This is where the "three Barbara's" stepped in. Barbara Puckett, Barbara Hall, and Barbara Harrell started a door-to-door campaign to sign up new members for SMPS. Within several months, the SMPS membership went from 69 to nearly 1500. They were tireless in their efforts. Likewise, Ty Law took our monthly newsletter and produced a new San Marco Times That was mailed to the new members, as well as being displayed in all the shops in San Marco Square. The membership brought SMPS political clout, and as we had our meetings in The Little Theatre, more and more politicians showed up to hear about this new community action.

The big conflict occurred when we rejected the city's proposed revitalization plan. Citing far too extensive damage to the merchants, many of them new, as well as the removal of substantial live oaks on Largo Rd, we wanted something far more phased and less onerous on the merchants and their survival. Meetings in The Little Theatre got heated at times, as the city laid out the scope of its plan, but the sympathy was coming the way of SMPS, as well as the political voice. Councilman Gifford Grange and Mayor Jake Godbold saw the momentum shifting, and backed SMPS. The newspaper also ran a top left hand editorial column, "The City should help, not hinder San Marco's revitalization". The plan would be modified to be phased in to protect the merchants, and to protect the adjoining neighborhoods.

With much of the revitalization weight now back on the shoulders of SMPS, it was time for us to act. With the city purchase of the old Gulf service station site, SMPS decided to raise money to build a centerpiece park on this site. After working with original designer, Andy Lilliskis, and his original plans, we developed a more intriguing park plan, and we started receiving budget numbers to build it ourselves. The best proposal came in at $250,000. So we went public, via our San Marco Times, to begin raising money within the community to build our centerpiece park. Much to our surprise, within a month of starting our big campaign, Mrs. Abla Balis, contacted us, having seen our Times article, and asked if we would name the park for her deceased husband, Sheffield Balis, if she funded the total amount. After some quick meetings of the board, her proposal was approved. Thus Balis Park would become the centerpiece and the momentum builder for the revitalization of the Square. Two years later the park became a reality.

I recall a Jacksonville Magazine cover from the mid-80's with a picture of old San Marco Square, and the caption, "Will San Marco Make It?" The late 80's proved to be the years that all this planning finally paid off, as street by street, the square began its makeover with new sidewalks, street lamps, planting, and of course, a beautiful Balis Park to capture the momentum.

Doug Alred – The Festival of Lights 5K, which is held in conjunction with Holiday Magic is the highlight of the Christmas season in the Square. Over 3,000 runners and a few thousand visitors attend this wonderful event. The evening opens with the arrival of Santa and Mrs. Claus as they parade around the Square on a large ladder truck provided by the Jacksonville Fire Department. After a tour of the Square, Santa and Mrs. Claus set up in the Gazebo to take pictures with the kids. The Square is decorated with thousands of white lights and Christmas music fills the air through speakers located throughout the center. There is a one mile fun run for the kids at 5:30pm. Each child finishing the fun run receives a custom designed medal. At 6pm the 5k run/walk kicks off from Atlantic Blvd. at the corner of Hendricks Avenue. The luminary lit course takes the runners and walkers down Hendricks to River Oaks Road and then follow River Road to San Marco Blvd. The course wraps around the Square and finishes on Atlantic Blvd in the Square. Participants often wear jingle bells on their shoes and there are lots of Christmas themed costumes.

After the 5K has finished, the Square comes alive with stilt-walkers dressed in Christmas costumes, a horse drawn hay ride, miniature train rides, face-painting, petting zoo, and lots of games for the kids. There is even be a snow-blow area to really get you in the Christmas spirit. Everyone is invited to browse around the Square and check out the retails shops and restaurants, which are open throughout the evening. Activities continue until 8:30pm. This event is designed to showcase the San Marco Square shopping area and also to help raise funds for the Children's Miracle Network.

Pat Andrews – "You can dream, create, design and build the most beautiful place in the world, but it requires people to make it a reality."   Walt Disney

Since 1926 San Marco residents have had a genuine sense of place and neighborhood. The community has a strong identity with physical surroundings worth caring about and worth preserving. More importantly, it has a collective interdependence of neighbors who respect and care for one another. Our surroundings have tree-lined streets, the St. Johns River, centrality to Jacksonville and a centerpiece, San Marco Square, the perfect neighborhood anchor for easy Friday nights, good shopping, eating, strolling and taking in a movie or play.

I am extremely fortunate to have called San Marco my home for 33 years. I give great credit to the San Marco Preservation Society for its vibrancy and dedicated effort to make the neighborhood dynamic and sustainable. Personally, I have worked with many neighbors on quality of life matters such as safety concerns, planning and growth issues, speed and traffic concerns, historical buildings and preservation of tree canopies and gardens. I was President of SMPS as we welcomed the gift of the shared Baptist Parking lot, the Ronald McDonald House and additions to our Merchant community such as Firehouse Subs!

So, Walt Disney didn't know it at the time, but he was talking about my home, San Marco. A community worth working for, living in and preserving, cohesively held together by folks that care about the quality of life and each other.

Janet Molyneaux, Mike Molyneaux, and Desiree Bailey – The San Marco Bookstore was opened in 1973 by the Blauer family. The space formerly housed a Rexall Pharmacy, but books soon filled the space, which makes the bookstore one of the few businesses that has operated in San Marco Square for nearly half of San Marco's existence. The Blauer family, John, Laura and their son Mike, were true book enthusiasts and led the store until 1999. Janet and Mike Molyneaux bought the store then and have made it a multi-generational bookstore for the last 17 years. Their daughter, Desiree Bailey, and Desiree's children Colin and Kate are often seen in the aisles. As time has passed and San Marco has changed, the San Marco Bookstore has changed too, no longer carrying vinyl records or dusty science text books. Instead, by adding the PAPYRUS greeting cards, expanding children's books, toys and gifts, and bringing in literary gifts, the store has grown to meet the needs of the neighborhood. Therefore, the bookstore is now known as **San Marco Books and More**. This community fixture carries old and new books, specializing in Jacksonville and Florida history, children's and classic literature and is sure to walk you down Memory Lane with their classic toys such as marbles, jacks and tiddlywinks! They have also re-published regional books of interest, including the North Florida Civil War account *Dickison and His Men* by Mary Elizabeth Dickison and Marjorie Kinnan Rawlings' *Secret River*. In addition, the bookstore regularly hosts local authors for signings and literary events. Featured guests include Mary Badham, the actress who portrayed "Scout" in the *To Kill a Mockingbird* film, local writers Wayne Wood and Mark Woods, and San Marco authors Charles Martin, Robin Robinson and Debra Webb Rogers. The bookstore even hosted a midnight release Harry Potter party that included a San Marco Square scavenger hunt, costume contest and butterbeer. Even the youngest of readers are welcomed as the bookstore hosts Story Time in Balis Park on the 2nd Saturday of each month.

The success and foundation of the bookstore is firmly rooted in the San Marco community. As past presidents of the San Marco Merchants Association (SMMA) and as a board member of the San Marco Preservation Society (SMPS), the bookstore strives to embrace and support our neighborhood. We thank you for your support; we look forward to the next ten years and the celebration of 100 years of San Marco!

Mike Balanky – When I was a teenager in the late 60's and early 70's my dad managed the Brinks Armored Car Service which was located at the intersection of Prudential Drive and Hendricks Avenue. There was a gas station across the street where Thai Bistro is today and BB's was a restaurant called the Thompson House. I remember eating many a plate of pancakes and perusing all of the Florida Gators paraphernalia on the walls.

Each weekend my brother and sister and I would come to Brinks and wash the armored trucks to earn extra spending money. Since I was the most agile I would usually end up washing the tops of the big cube trucks. I remember sitting up there and looking out at the beautiful St. Johns river and thinking what a great place it would be to live right there on the river. I mused about how cool it would be to be in walking distance to San Marco Square, Downtown and the "Gator Bowl". I never imagined that nearly 40 years later I would be living on that very same piece of property at the top of San Marco Place condominiums. And my mom and dad are in the very same building!

San Marco has always been a great neighborhood but I believe its best days are still ahead. A new mixed-use Publix supermarket will break ground soon and The District 30 acre riverfront development will be transformational. Several other mixed use developments are in the planning stages and a new transit oriented development is in the pipeline as well.

The people who live in San Marco are fiercely proud of their neighborhood and for good reason. Home sales are some of the most stable in the city with a variety of price points from first time homeowners to riverfront McMansions. The incredible coastline, historic architecture and central location will continue to attract a dynamic diversity of young families, urbanites, and empty nesters.

Gayle and I and our two golden-doodles are proud to be part of the fabric of San Marco.

Kris Barnes – My father, Robert Charles Broward, was born March 30, 1926 and brought home to their house on Louisa Street. His father, Pulaski Broward, was the chief engineer on the ferryboat *Fletcher* that traveled between the South and North banks of the St. Johns River. My grandfather built a home at the corner of Hendricks Avenue and River Oaks Road around 1930 where my father grew up with his siblings.

He went to Georgia Tech to study Architecture, did a fellowship with Frank Lloyd Wright and then returned to Jacksonville in 1953 where he worked with various architects until he opened his own practice in 1956. This office was in the upstairs of what now houses Indochine restaurant.

Over the years he moved his office to different locations but in 1965 he bought an old run down house at 1922 Felch Avenue and renovated it for his office. Over the next 15 years he bought the properties on either side of him and created a studio complex that housed other architects and engineers.

I took over the property in June of 2011 when he could no longer go into the office and renovated it re-opening in April of 2013 for tenants.

He wrote two books about Henry John Klutho, the architect who designed many of the buildings during the rebuilding of Jacksonville after the 1901 fire. The first was The Architecture of Henry John Klutho the Prairie School in Jacksonville (1983) and the second was a revised second edition of the same title (2003). He also wrote a book about our family history, *The Broward Family from France to Florida 1764-2011* which was published by the Jacksonville Historical Society. He was awarded the State of Florida Artist Hall of Fame in 2012 being only the second architect to be honored as such.

Jan Bebeau – Festival d'Vine, one of the major fundraising events for Catholic Charities, began in San Marco Square in 2004. A volunteer with Catholic Charities, Margo Kelly, had recently moved from Atlanta to Jacksonville and offered to organize a wine tasting event inspired by the High Museum wine event in Atlanta. Margo was introduced to Chad Munsey, who owned the Grotto, and he suggested that if the event was held in San Marco, he would coordinate with wine distributors to donate and pour wine during the Festival. Margo and Cindy Baker, another volunteer, met with San Marco restaurateurs who willingly agreed to support the event by donating and serving food at the Festival. Charles Johnston, owner of Helena View Johnston Vineyards, was the first featured vintner for Festival d'Vine. He is the father of Sara Marie Johnston, longtime resident and owner of San Marco's new Town Hall Restaurant. Scott Riley, owner of Stellers Gallery, generously opened up his art gallery where Catholic Charities held a silent auction. The first event in Balis Park was attended by approximately 350 people. The popularity of the event and number of attendees outgrew San Marco Square, so in 2012 Treaty Oak Park became the new home of Festival d'Vine. It has been held at Treaty Oak Park for the past 5 years and has continued to be a huge success. The Festival continues to be supported by the San Marco community and recent Festivals have been attended by over 850 people.

The proceeds of Festival d'Vine have always been directed to the Catholic Charities Emergency Assistance Program. The goal of this program is to help prevent homelessness by providing rent, utilities and food to families in our community who are experiencing
financial crisis.

Jan Bebeau, Georgia Dahl, Suzanne Perritt – San Marco Garden Circle - Passion and Energy

The SMGC was founded in 1932 with 17 women who shared a love for flowers, beautification and community service. As we celebrate our 85 years, our membership has increased but remains diverse, vibrant and passionate. We continue to carry on many of the traditions established over the years. We are a circle that has cultivated long friendships and an unwavering devotion to one another while working closely together on projects.

One such project being Adopt.A.Park. In 1991, SMGC developed Historic Kings Road Park, formerly Fulton Green at Times Square" located at the intersection of Atlantic Blvd and Kings Road. Several hundred citizens were in attendance for the dedication including, celebrity guest, Martha Stewart, who assisted in the ribbon cutting, along with Councilwoman Ginny Myrick. State representative, Joe Arnold, local city of Jacksonville dignitaries, honored guests as well as many residents were in attendance to witness this historic occasion. Historic Kings Road Park recognizes the original Spanish

Trade Route and the first road for vehicular traffic that ran along the Henry Flagler Railroad down the east coast of Florida.

The San Marco Garden Circle received numerous awards for this endeavor including: the Deep South Traveling Trophy, the Historic Preservation Restoration Award, the May Duff Walters Trophy for Preservation of Beauty, the Civic Beautification Project Award, a City of Jacksonville Certificate of Appreciation and the Florida Federation Commercial Plant Award. In 1993 San Marco Preservation Society honored SMPS with the Beautification Award- "recognizing outstanding contributions to the development and rehabilitation of San Marco neighborhood".

Other San Marco Garden Circle contributions include:

1989- Balis Park Christmas Decorations-SMGC began their annual decoration of Balis Park, including the Christmas Tree and wreathes for the lampposts, awarded Madira Bickel Civic Achievement Award District IV

1990- Creation of the Live Nativity, at the home of Susan Fields - Arbor Lane, with Judy Blumberg and Muriel Parks

1993- Noel House- Southern Hospitality Dinner and entertainment at home of Judge and Mrs. Donald Moran of River Road. Sold out crowd for two nights

1995- Noel House- Old English Christmas themed dinner and entertainment at the home of Deborah Barnes - Brookwood Rd

1995- Official adoption of the Rose Garden at Landon Park (Adopt.A.Park project) from the City of Jacksonville, awarded a Civic Beautification Award as well as the highly honorable Eva Noble Award, which recognizes the Outstanding Circle of the Year

1995- General Norman Schwarzkopf Reception at the beautiful riverfront home of Georgia Dahl, where together we created an air of southern hospitality with beautiful floral arrangements and desserts

1996- Noel House- Olde English Dicken's Christmas at the home of Deborah Barnes

1996- Dahl Dude Ranch- A neighborhood party for the American Cancer Society at the Dahl home which raised $15,000 to help stomp out cancer

1996 - Noel House at Debbie Barnes home, sold out, one night event

May 16, 2006- Dedication celebration of the Rose Garden in Landon Park

2007- Developed and maintained a Butterfly Garden at Hendricks Elementary School, a program for which the students are now taking responsibility

2010- Puckett's Patch- a vegetable garden donated to Riverside Presbyterian Day School for the students to experience gardening, in honor of SMGC's Barbara Denmark Puckett

2011- Traditional Lighting of the Christmas Tree in Balis Park- a new tradition began with the lighting of the tree bringing the community together to celebrate the festivities of the season

The Jacksonville Garden Club Garden Tours- provided homes, gardens and hostesses for the many garden Club Garden Club Tours throughout the city

Preservation Hall- In conjunction with the City of Jacksonville and San Marco Preservation Society, we relocated the Carpenter Gothic Church from the Museum of Science and History property to Atlantic Boulevard's Fletcher Park. Provided a reception celebration for the event as well as necessary landscaping and funds for beautification

Duval County Extension Office Canning Kitchen we produced and sold Brunswick Stew, corn relish, bread and butter pickles, cranberry apple chutney and caramel sauce, all complete with personalized labels

Easter Floral Sale*
Christmas Greenery Sale*
Mother's Day Luncheon at Preservation Hall*

*These and other SMGC projects generated funds that went toward the beautification of neighborhood parks as well as throughout the Jacksonville Community

Military Support- The San Marco Garden Circle provided care packages to local servicemen serving in the Middle East and funds to the Seabees to purchase gloves and other needed supplies

Philanthropic Outreach- we have provided food, books and supplies to various organizations including the Salvation Army, Clara White Mission, Hubbard House, Ronald McDonald House, Catholic Charities Food Pantry, St. Francis Animal Hospital and the San Marco Fire Station

Robert Blade – We moved to Jacksonville in August of 1974 and found a little house to rent in Arlington. Three years later, just after Christmas, the owner, who was in the Navy, decided to retire and wanted his house back. We—my wife, Anna, and I, and our three young children—set off on a house search. We saw nothing we liked until the day the real estate agent took us to San Marco, to show us a house on Broadmoor Lane, pricier than what we wanted, but within reach. The house was a two-story red brick that looked a little eccentric. Anna stepped in the front door that day, took in the warm rooms, the gentle staircase going upstairs, the wonderful feel of the place, and said, "This is it. We have to buy this one."

"Um, don't you want to look around first?" I said. "I will, but I already know," she said. "This is it." We paid the owners exactly what they were asking (Anna didn't want to chance someone sneaking in ahead of us). And that was that. In early March 1978, we moved in and have had no regrets. Beyond the house there were two green parks, then San Marco Square in easy walking distance: Peterson's five and dime and Pic N' Save, a used book store and a comic book and record shop. They are all gone, of course. But the house is the constant. It has seen our family laugh and cry, rage and love, celebrate and mourn. It has offered us place for a rich, full, varied life, rooted in the past, in our memories, and still looking to the future.

David Blue – San Marco has seen so much change through the years it would be hard to chronicle. Shops, restaurants, service providers come and go. Mims, Geisenhof's, Carl West's Gulf Station- the list is long. Throughout time, the landmark consistency has been "The Little Theatre" and the resplendent (such modesty on my part) "San Marco Theatre". My wife and I have been the proud proprietors of the San Marco for the past 20 years and feel that the old girl will be around for many more. When we took it over it was running sub-run films with the most popular night being Wednesday when it was "No Smoking". We remember fondly taking down the bronze light fixtures only to find out they were actually silver the bronze tinge was actually the accumulation of fifteen years of nicotine. The good old days. We have customers that have been with us through the whole journey and we are extraordinarily grateful for the support that the San Marco community has always provided.

I think that the neon "San Marco" has to be one of the most photographed icons in Jacksonville. I strongly suspect that the second most photographed site is the brick wall that runs along Balis. Fashion shoots, children's photos of significant milestones in their young lives and endless engagement shots. We are happy to provide a backdrop for so many memories.

Just in our tenure we have seen so much change, and it has always been for the better. Balis Park, the three lions fountain, the new street lights- again, the list is long. At the end of the day you have to acknowledge that the success of San Marco Square and its surrounding neighborhood is a vibrant tribute to countless hours of deep-felt care and the effort of countless volunteers. The San Marco Preservation Society has been a bulwark in protecting its turf and providing a long range vision. We have very much enjoyed the ride and look forward to being part of the community for years to come.

Zim Boulos – It was 1994 and I had just finished refereeing a soccer game in Denver. Our post-game meal was in Larimer Square, which is Denver's oldest and most historic neighborhood. The old buildings along the square had become home to an inspired mix of independent shops, chef-driven restaurants and lively bars and clubs. Soon I started thinking our own San Marco square might just have this same kind of potential.

At a San Marco Preservation Society board meeting a few months later, we were discussing the merits of repairing the old tiered "wedding cake" fountain that was sinking on one side. The foundation of the fountain was failing and the design was lagging behind the rest of the square which was evolving into a more vital retail and functionally diverse environment. I had seen a large pineapple-style fountain in Charleston, South Carolina, which had become a focal point and a community gathering place. Local children ran and played in the nearby water while the parents relaxed and visited with each other. Why couldn't we have something like that in Jacksonville? I proposed organizing a competition to design a new fountain. Six months later an appointed committee that reviewed over 30 entries and eventually selected the husband and wife team of architects Alan Wilson and Angela Shifanella. Their beautiful design featured the three lions and the campanile, or bell tower.

The next step was fundraising. The main donors who supported our efforts were Lori Boyer, Wayne and Kitty Davis, Jimmy and Benita Boyd, and Bob Davis. Jacksonville City Council member Ginny Myrick arranged for city matching funds and we were on our way as trusted stewards of a challenging project. A few weeks later we commissioned Florida sculptor Hugh Nicholson to execute the project. He had created a successful bronze sculpture of manatees at the

Governor's mansion in Tallahassee. My wife Terry, who is a part of all these projects, along with Alan and Angela, made many trips to his studio and spent long hours working with the artist to achieve the caliber of exacting detail and overall vision which was ultimately realized in the lions as we experience them today. I'll never forget the astounding transformation from a seven inch rough model to the monumental bronze sculpture that has since become an iconic symbol of the San Marco community.

The new fountain was unveiled on April 18, 1997, at the Carnevale di San Marco celebration that attracted more than 3,000 attendees. Every time I see kids exploring the park and families posing for photos on it, it puts a smile on my face.

I hope people never lose sight of the importance of public art and the invaluable role it plays in good urban design and historic preservation. Just as it has over centuries, public art also stirs the spirit, awakens and inspires our creativity and serves as link to the past across multiple generations. As I have traveled, I have seen many examples of great public art, and some we've brought back to our city:

- "The Jester," which is located right in front of Theater Jax, and celebrates the oldest continuously running community theater in the country. Making it possible were Theater Jax, Keith and Joyce Kimball, Rob and Linda Larkin Smith, Bob Smith, Tyree and Lori Boyer, RJ Nemeyer, Wayne and Kitty Davis, Eddie Fink, and Terry, Zim and Meredith Boulos.

- "The Stilt Walkers" in the traffic circle at The Museum of Science and History. This is my favorite piece, as it can be viewed in the round. When I first saw it in Vail,

Colorado I knew it would be perfect for The MOSH. Thanks to Peter and LeeAnn Rummell and Office Environments & Services. City Council member Reggie Fullwood was instrumental in securing public funding.

- "The Kite Kids," located in Balis Park, turned out to be a favorite of the children of San Marco, and I love witnessing their delight as they explore the park and interact with the sculpture. City Council member Matt Carlucci secured the funding for this sculpture.

- "Journey to the Imagination," located in front of The Wardroom Ltd., depicts a boy daydreaming and riding on a paper airplane. It reminds us all of the value of dreams. This sculpture was made possible by Jimmy and Benita Boyd.

In addition to the public art, there were many other San Marco improvement projects over the past 20 years, which were brainstormed and executed with a foundation committee that included me, Lori Boyer, Rob Smith, and Keith Kimball. Elimination of power lines in the area opened the way for better vistas and a major sidewalk renovation was undertaken (inspired by a conversation I had with Andres Duane, distinguished urban planner who was instrumental in the planning of the award-winning Seaside Village), Street trees, traditional street light fixtures, a bus shelter, and a clock for the square (thank you, Saltmarsh family). The much needed renovation plan of the fire station was designed by Angela Shifanella and with the help of Larry Peterson. As is evidenced in the paver inscriptions, bench memorials, and including the invisible contributors, it required the mighty village of San Marco to make this dream a reality. Karen Franklin's unique

44

touch is seen in the signage in and around the square. Council member George Banks secured significant funding for many of these projects.

We also had help from two of our city's outstanding mayors. John Peyton almost single-handedly pushed through the successful renovation of San Marco Boulevard, and John Delaney and Sam Mousa of his staff were invaluable in their support of the renovation of Hendricks Avenue and the surrounding square. Doug Skiles was the civil engineering guru who designed and executed the plan to reroute traffic, thus improving flow and doubling the square's public space.

San Marco is truly a special place filled with caring and committed people. It's a place I've lived almost all my life, and it holds so many precious memories. My very first memory of San Marco is as a four-year-old boy eating a slice of peanut butter pie outside Mim's Bakery (currently, Taverna) in 1959. Decades later I would take my own four year old to the square to ride the coin-operated green whale, which rested just outside the Pic 'N' Save discount store. She is an adult now, living in another state and becoming a physician, but her memories of growing up in rare and wonderful San Marco will be carried with her wherever she goes. I don't know whatever became of the green whale.

Benita & Jimmy Boyd – The Happy days being a child in San Marco.

The 1400 block of LaRue Ave was a wonderful area; six little girls lived on that block all within 2 years apart. There were boys too, but they were older and we didn't play with them. What fun we would have on Saturdays walking up San

45

Marco Blvd to go to the San Marco Theatre. Sometimes we would walk in the median and sometimes on the sidewalk. Our Mamas would give us the appropriate change to see the movie as well as for a box of popcorn. Often times our mothers would be allowed in the theater to tap us on the shoulder and tell us it was time to go.

Also, we lived across from what we called the playground. It was the playground for Southside Grammar School Number 7 which was located on Flagler. The neighborhood boys would get together for pickup game of baseball. Our father was affiliated with the baseball team named the Jacksonville Tars. The boys liked Mr. Boyd as he would bring balls, bats and gloves for them to play with and gave them pointers on the game.

After Christmas the boys would ride their bicycles all over the greater neighborhood collecting the discarded Christmas trees. They would bring them to the playground and stack them up. The little girls would check them out to see that all the ornaments had been removed. Tinsel was a big find as it was during WWII and tin foil was a very precious commodity. At some designated time the neighbors would gather around the trees and then the trees would be set on fire. Sounds a little pagan now!

My brother, Jimmy, remembers trying to fly kites at the park, going to the San Marco Theatre, having ice cream at the corner store. But best of all, our mothers would go to the A&P grocery store and Mr. Walker, the head bag man, would take Mamas groceries to the car allowing us to ride in the buggy to the car. The parking was so tight that often times he would have to back the cars out for the ladies.

46

Those were wonderful times grow up in. Some of us from that street are still friends after all these years.

Lori Boyer – I moved to San Marco from Avondale in 1987 and fell in love with the neighborhood's historic charm, welcoming neighbors, and wonderful sense of community. Living on the site the former Villa Alexandria, and having been active in San Marco Preservation Society and San Marco Garden Circle for nearly 30 years, my stories could fill an entire book but some of my favorite memories date from the late 1980's and 1990's.

The holidays remain a special time in San Marco but in the 80's and 90's they were spectacular. Holiday Magic, held in early December, was a bustling event that drew thousands of residents from more than just the neighborhood. All the shops were open serving hot chocolate, cider and other treats to those who dropped by. There was a petting zoo and horse drawn carriage rides, and Santa arrived by sleigh or fire engine to the delight of the children. Balis Gazebo was graced by an enormous live tree donated from Oaklawn Cemetery, and holiday music played throughout the Square on lamppost speakers. Hand bell choirs and carolers joined in the festivities and the evening was truly one not to be missed. The luminaria later in the month included almost every lot in the entire area and was breathtaking. The live nativity even included a camel! And the Bi-annual Holiday Tour of Homes not only featured beautiful homes decked out for the season, but hundreds of friends and neighbors volunteered to staff the tour and hospitality tents. The streets were filled with residents walking from home to home, chatting with old friends and making new ones. It was truly a joyous and heartwarming experience that was woven into the fabric of the community.

While the construction of the clay courts at Southside Park and the new Lion Fountain in the Square were major events of the era, I think perhaps the move of San Marco Preservation Hall from its prior home next to MOSH to its present location in Fletcher Park in 1994 was one of the most exciting. Constructed as St. Paul's Episcopal Church in the late 1800's, the carpenter gothic style building was already a historic landmark, but stood in the way of expansion plans for MOSH. San Marco Preservation took on the project of relocating the building. The move was a planning and engineering feat. You may think I am referring to the structural challenges of moving a 100 year building without destroying it- but the real issues were surrounded how to get it off the site and to its new home. There was no way to get off the MOSH site by road without going under an overpass and they were all too short for the former church. So the church was rolled on timbers to a barge waiting in Friendship Park and began its journey up river under the Fuller Warren Bridge. It was rolled back ashore at Cedar Street and loaded on a flatbed truck. But the difficulties did not stop there- the next obstacle course to maneuver involved overhead power lines. While a few had to be lowered along the way and the route was circuitous eventually travelling down Kings to Atlantic and then back to the Park, the cost and outage impacts were minimized, and the move was a success! It was a day filled with adventure for the hundreds of residents who followed the journey or lined the streets to watch the historic structure pass by.

Tyrie W. Boyer – San Marco from a Junior High Perspective

When I was a youngster, the Southside was everything from the Southside Shipyards to Mandarin. In those days, from the north, San Marco started at about Landon Ave. and ended on the south at River Oaks Rd. There was a cute little shopping area in the middle which is still there.

Nowadays I regularly see houses advertised "for sale in San Marco" as far south as what we always referred to as "Lakewood." By 1960 my family had moved from Cesery Blvd. in Arlington to a house between San Marco and Lakewood in a community known as Granada.

Although at that time I never claimed to be a resident of San Marco, I spent a lot of time there. Landon was both a middle and high school and that is where I started in the seventh grade. However, since the city limits of Jacksonville ended at Greenridge Road (before consolidation), we did not have school bus transportation. We caught the city bus for $.10 each way. Every morning and every afternoon the city buses were full of youngsters going to and from school. We could catch either 31 Colonial Manor or 41 Lakewood bus.

We were dropped off in front of the San Marco Theater and walked from there to Landon. In the afternoons we walked back to the theater and caught the bus from there. While we waited for the bus, we would wander the square. Other than the theater, I can think of no other store that is the same as in 1960.

At one end of San Marco was Setzer's, a food store. In close proximity was Barnett Jewelers. The Town Pump was located where Indochine is now and Mims bakery was next door. Down a little ways was White's Bookstore next to the theater while across the street was Peterson's 5 and 10 Cent Store. Utsey's was a shoe store where my mother bought Buster Browns for my younger brother. It was next to The Young Men's Shop, a clothing store, and across the street from a bowling alley. Originally it was a regular bowling alley but later changed to something called "duckpin bowling."

There was a Banner food store in San Marco as well as two or three filling stations where attendants pumped the gas, washed the windshields and swept the floors of our cars. We also had a tire store where Firehouse Subs is now located, and on the same side of that street was a laundromat with "atomic dry cleaning."

When I lived in Arlington, the children would walk to the theater on Saturdays and pay $.10 to get in. When we moved to the Southside we had to pay a quarter to get into the San Marco Theater. (That's 250% inflation!) However, the cost of popcorn, $.10 a bag, was the same at both places.

In junior high, boys and girls would go steady. That meant that they were "in love" and each would have only one boyfriend or girlfriend. The way to advertise the relationship was for the boy to give his high school ring to the girl. However, if you were in junior high, you did not own a ring. That problem was solved with the boy giving the girl his sterling silver ID bracelet.

I wanted to go steady with a girl named Cindy, but I did not own an ID bracelet. I was not about to tell my intentions to my parents, so, on my own, I went to Barnett Jewelers in San Marco and met with Oscar Barnett. He helped me find the bracelet I could afford. With my hard earned money from mowing and raking yards, I bought a bracelet which could be engraved for $.10 per letter. To save some money I only had my first name carved into the silver.

Unfortunately, it took some time for me to earn the money to pay for the bracelet. By the time I got it, Cindy was going steady with somebody else. Believe it or not, when I was cleaning some chests of drawers about a year ago, I found that bracelet. It is tarnished now but could easily be cleaned up if sterling ID bracelets come back in style. Maybe I will save it for one of my grandsons.

Because of girls or for some other good reason, it was not unusual for boys at Landon to get in shoving matches while at school. If the coaches heard about it, they would arrange for differences to be settled with boxing gloves during gym classes. The gloves were heavy and heavily padded and the boys would be exhausted in short order. Another solution was for the principal to give each boy a swat with a wooden paddle.

If neither of those solutions worked, the boys would set up secret meetings behind Petersons 5 and 10. Word would get around and there would be plenty of kids there to watch and make certain that there was no dirty fighting. When somebody said "enough" the tussle would cease. By the next day, the principal always knew about those get-togethers and arrangements were once again made for each participant to get another swat.

Like San Marco, times have changed. To be sure, I do not recommend fighting and I am sure that today the boys would, at best, be suspended and at worst expelled. Amazingly, after those fights it was not unusual for the participants to become good, if not best, of friends.

In fact, they might meet back in San Marco and go duckpin bowling together.

Forrest V. Brewer – I spent most of my early life on the Westside of Jacksonville in the Riverside, Avondale, Ortega areas. As a young adult, I spent several years in Winter Park, Florida.

I was exposed to San Marco through an aunt who lived on Pineridge Road. When I would visit her I was intrigued by the area. I loved the architecture, the parks, the wide streets, but most importantly, the people.

In 1978 I left Winter Park and moved back to Jacksonville, and chose San Marco as my new neighborhood.

Those were incredible days; young people were moving in and making a difference. Most of the new residents were young professionals with little money. There was a lot of "sweat equity". We painted, repaired windows, resurfaced wooden floors, whatever it took. People worked together, shared tools, shared ideas, and we knew everyone in the neighborhood.

This community spirit spread and soon we were taking on the parks, the square, sidewalks, and alleys. We often had "Cleanup Campaigns" targeting an area for a clean sweep.

We also were aware of crime! Living in an urban area meant caution and awareness. We started a Neighborhood Watch and later a Security Association.

Jacksonville was a huge city and we knew that we could not depend on the city government for everything so we just pitched in and did things ourselves.

Later came the San Marco Preservation Society and

even greater accomplishments. We all joined and enjoyed the social aspects of the organization. We had great speakers, special events and covered dish suppers.

San Marco became "the neighborhood"; we were the envy of every other neighborhood in the city. We accomplished great things by being united.

Soon the Square started perking! New businesses, restaurants and lots of remodeling. The residents supported the local businesses. We would not think of going anywhere else. The Square began shaping into what it is today.

I look back at these days with great nostalgia, but I know in my heart, the best days are ahead. As long as we continue with our great community spirit, we can conquer all.

Sarah Boone – Theatre Jacksonville was founded almost a century ago in 1919 as The Community Players and, in 1926, joined the nationwide "little theater" movement to become The Little Theatre of Jacksonville. In 1938, a generous donation from Jacksonville cigar magnate Carl Swisher enabled The Little Theatre to build a playhouse in the heart of San Marco where the group has resided ever since. Ivan Smith, a founding partner of Reynolds, Smith and Hills architecture firm, designed the playhouse that just over fifty years later was placed on the National Register of Historic Places. It's hard to believe given the bustling activity in the square today, but picture San Marco Blvd just before World War II with only the Little Theatre and the San Marco Movie Theatre as the major entertainment destinations in the Square.

In 1972, the Theatre changed its name to Theatre Jacksonville to better reflect its community-wide role and over the years has adapted to the changing entertainment landscape, embracing technology, expanding its community outreach and developing a robust agenda that includes high-quality performances, performing arts education and training and extensive community collaborations. Beyond its many contributions to Jacksonville and Northeast Florida, Theatre Jacksonville contributes to the national theater field by producing talent that enjoys success far beyond the local market. Among those nationally recognized artists who count Theatre Jacksonville as part of their training are Emmy award winning TV/film/Broadway actor Michael Emerson, TV/film actor Tyler Ross, TV/Broadway actress Emily Swallow and Broadway music director Joey Chancey. Theatre Jacksonville is proud to be an anchor institution at the south end of San Marco Square. As we gear up for our 100 year anniversary, all of us at the Theatre are thrilled to celebrate San Marco's 90th year milestone. We look forward to our continuing partnerships with all San Marco friends and neighbors. #SeeYouAtTheTheatre.

Captain J M Broxson Jr. RN EMT-P – I consider myself very lucky to have been introduced to San Marco early in my life. As a young boy, I would often visit my father who worked at the local fire station. Dad always told me how special this community was and how close he felt to the residents. I followed in the family business, being assigned to Fire Station 13 in 1996 and I've grown attached to the area.

San Marco possesses the charm of a small town. Even though we're in the heart of the city, the pedestrian feel of the area lends itself to gathering together and slowing down a little.

Smiles and waves come much easier, even for unfamiliar faces. Shopkeepers often know their customers and each other by name. Local residents bring their children to see the firetrucks and it's not uncommon to see young adults who were toddlers when we first met. It's one of those areas that once you visit, you never want to leave.

A busy area on workdays, San Marco changes after hours and on weekends. The bustle of downtown commuter traffic ebbs and gives way to strollers, skateboards, and bicycles. The locals come out to enjoy the restaurants, theaters, and street performers. Many people just come out to sit beside the fountain or walk the dogs. On weekends and holidays, there are frequent art shows to crowd the streets or seasonal displays adorning the gazebo. The square is rarely lacking of some local talent grabbing a guitar and entertaining the passing crowds. After hours, with few exceptions, the square is remarkably quiet and peaceful. At two or three in the morning, it seems the lions have reclaimed the park.

The community has an impressive resilience that has weathered growth and decay. During the last economic downturn, signs of recession were common but never took hold. New developments slowed or stopped, some businesses closed, and the numbers of business patrons seemed to dwindle but, the spirit of San Marco persevered. Now with the growth returning, businesses are opening, construction projects are numerous, and even a new traffic pattern was introduced to the square but the local charm remains.

Crowds have returned to the sidewalk cafes and shops but it's not crowded. Removal of the traffic lights has improved the flow of vehicles and marked crosswalks have improved the pedestrian experience. It seems that San Marco is impervious to the effects of feast or famine.

My favorite aspect of San Marco is the people. The families I meet, the shopkeepers, the residents, and the visitors. This community is so warm and engaging, it's difficult to not become attached at some level. The residents take ownership of this area and its reputation, and it makes one want to be a part of it. The people always seem to put their best foot forward and it's a beautiful community.

Ryan Buckley – As the proprietor of Gallery Framery on the square, I had the opportunity to be involved in five San Marco Art Festivals. I've always felt that San Marco Square is an amazing location for this type of event, with its park, statues, and distinctive architecture. Some years have seen as many as 20,000 visitors for the show. Starting in the Mid 90s, the Festival was run for almost two decades by *Howard Alan Events* based out of Jupiter, Florida. Local promotion company, *Events by Jamie*, also ran two shows in the 2000s.
As part of my involvement in the show I selected artists to create a print commemorating that year's event. Ray Brilli, Gary Mack, Kathy Frosio, and Nancy Asbell all created beautiful San Marco scenes during the early 2000s. Local middle school student, Regan Foote, also created the official poster for the show in 2009.

The range of artists in the show has always been fantastic and includes sculptors, watercolorists, oil painters, glass blowers, and jewelers, to name a few. I've always felt that this type of cultural event is an important component of a healthy community and a valuable asset to our San Marco neighborhood. I know the show is on temporary hiatus right now, but have high hopes for its return to beautiful San Marco in the near future.

Matt Carlucci Sr. – My memories of San Marco go back to my birth. I grew up in San Marco on Avoca place in a small 3 bedroom, 1 bath bungalow. No central air conditioning until high school. I loved our home. It was snug and sunny. My memories go back to climbing the red bud tree in the front yard and catching minnows with my big brother Michael and grandfather at the "creek" in Whatley Park. Back then it was not as manmade. There was a green wooden arched bridge over the creek filled with "elephant ears" and a beautiful willow tree at the bend. My mother took me to the park and we climbed a tree and made wishes. I suppose a lot of them came true as I have been blessed beyond what I deserve. It was our "wishing tree". I went to kindergarten at South Jacksonville Presbyterian and my teacher was sweet, beautiful and had the perfect name, Mrs. Apple. There was a bowling alley in the square and dad would takes us there as a family sometimes. Also an A&P grocery store where my grandmother would buy groceries and there was a coffee bean grinder at the end of the check out. I can still smell the coffee. Speaking of my grandmother, who lived on Belote Pl., she opened my first savings account at the old American Bank with a dollar fifty! Growing older I would ride my bike to the Coley-Walker drugstore. They had the best cheese burgers, crinkle fries and cherry cokes at the diner! I enjoyed the matinees at San Marco Theatre. Then there was Petersons 5 and dime store where I would buy model cars, fire crackers and smoke bombs. What else could a little boy ask for? It seemed the winters were colder then. We would take big pieces of card board and ride them down the hill at the park slope near Southside United Methodist church when the winter freezes made the grass brown and dry. Living in San Marco

57

allowed me to attend the beloved Hendricks Ave School and play ball at HAB. We were "The Boys of 66"!! My best friend from childhood, David Elian, and I would go fishing at Craig Creek every chance we could get! I also have great memories of "Thrill Hill" and training my first retriever in Lake Marco. I still live in San Marco, a block from where I grew up, with my wife Karen, on Alexandria Pl. So. We have 2 sons and their families living and working within a mile of our home. Our first little home was on Belote Pl. We would sit on the front steps and drink coffee after dinner, talk and, in the fall, smell coffee wafting over from Maxwell House plant thanks to the cool northeast winds. I could go on and on. Let me just say, San Marco was the best place a youngster could make memories, even if we did not have all the amenities we take for granted now. God Bless this wonderful community and the sweet people who make its fabric so special, then, now and for future generations to come!

Dr. Kelly Coker-Daniel – As a child, Landon High School was simply the school our family attended. My great aunt, Helen Tresca Golden (of the old Tresca the Florist on Atlantic Boulevard), was the first generation in our family to attend Landon as a graduate in the 1940s. My mother and father, Fran Peacock Coker and Howard Coker, were high school sweethearts and members of Landon's last graduating class of 1965. In addition, I have other aunts, uncles, cousins and family friends, too numerous to count, who also attended Landon.

Fifteen years into my service with Duval County Public Schools, I was given the opportunity in 2007 to be the principal of Landon at which time I became the third generation in my family to walk the same halls that my parents had walked as high school students. At the time, Landon was struggling academically and many San Marco families had opted to use other educational routes for their children. Working collectively with parents and community leaders, we converted Landon to a dedicated magnet middle school with a focus on advanced academics and leadership development.

While the main school building that is so familiar to San Marco residents was built in the 1920's, Landon's neighborhood roots go much deeper. The school's namesake, Julia Landon, was a teacher in the late 1800's in a one room school house located on the current school site. To honor its history and celebrate a new chapter, we decided to rename the school Julia Landon College Preparatory and Leadership Development School or, as nicknamed by the students, "JLCP" for short!

From the start, the San Marco community embraced the program changes. Parents began to enroll their children and the community businesses and organizations were quick to offer their time and support. I heard from countless alumni about how much Landon meant to them and I realized just how important JLCP was, and is, to past and present San Marco residents. As a result of the overwhelming community support, JLCP now consistently ranks as one of the top middle schools in the state.

Several years after I arrived, I was incredibly blessed to watch as my daughter and nephew enrolled as students and become the fourth generation of our family to be a part of the Landon community. While I have been fortunate to move on and serve our school district in other capacities, when I think back on the time spent at JLCP and the many wonderful children and supportive families I encountered during my time there, I cannot help but smile and be thankful to have had the opportunity to be a part of this amazing community.

Andy Cordek – Hendricks Avenue Elementary
Christmas Tree Lot

Whenever I think about the Christmas tree lot, I mostly think about my personal experiences there and the relationships that were started there or were nurtured there. The tree lot has been there as long as we have lived in San Marco (1994), but as I learned while loading trees for my neighbors, it has been around much longer than that. I loaded one tree for a gentleman who was there with his grandchildren, and he was telling me that he had loaded trees a generation before me. That sounded like a family tradition to me.

When I volunteered to work at the lot and started signing up for time slots, I was primarily thinking about how much money we were going to make in order to help fund the school patrol trip to Washington D.C... Before I knew it, the week of Thanksgiving had arrived, and so had the trailer full of Christmas trees. If I remember correctly, we decided to empty the trailer on Wednesday after school. It's not like unloading pumpkins at the patch, but it was hard work, I was sweating in spite of the cold weather, and I had a sore back for several days. I think I was trying to show off and hurt myself.

My first shift was Friday after Thanksgiving and ended up working an extra shift, but time flew by as we spread holiday cheer helping neighbors to decorate their homes for the holidays. By the end of the first hour, I regretted not bringing my work gloves...Oh well. When I got home that night, I remember shaking pine needles out of my jacket and hair. I spent a lot of time at the sink trying to remove the pine sap. All for a good cause, I told myself.

When I went back the next day, I was eager to get to work and really enjoyed getting to know the other patrol parents with whom I would be going to D.C. We would help our neighbors pick out the perfect tree and load it onto their car, wishing them a Merry Christmas and thanks for supporting the patrols.

Two years later, as the president of the patrol parents support association, I was concerned that we might not choose to run the lot again, but in the end, and with the support of the friends I had made from the last time, we ran another successful Christmas tree lot and earned money to support our children in their extra-curricular activity. I realize now, as I did then, that many more parents and children in the San Marco community share a common bond in making an annual tradition that many of our neighbors look forward to each year. Merry Christmas

Alice Coughlin – In 1958, my husband, Warren and I, and our two children, Cyndi and Mark, moved to Jacksonville. We knew very little about the city nor did we know anyone. We rented a house in St. Nicholas to be close to Assumption School. Our reason for moving here was the purchase of a small business that was located on San Marco Blvd, ·It wasn't long before we had definitely outgrown the space so we built a building in the Southside Industrial Park ...... and a home in San Jose Forest. Eventually, we built a beautiful home in Deerwood, then moved to a condo at Lakewood, then moved to a home on the river in Mandarin. Loved every place we have lived, always making wonderful friends whose friendship I treasure today.

I guess every ten years or so it was time to build a new home. Some think I'm crazy but I do love designing and building. In 2001, we made a decision to move again. This time it was making the full circle and going back to San Marco where we built once again. Yes, back where we started our life in Jacksonville. I do *love* it so as did Warren until he passed away in 2008. It is the most *fabulous* and friendly neighborhood. I love seeing so many of my neighbors walking, riding their bikes, pushing the strollers with their little ones ... waving to me with a friendly smile. Before Warren died, he suffered with Dementia ... he would walk to the Square, my knowing he was alright as our friendly merchants knew him, as did our Police... all keeping an eye on him... what a great area to live in. I am so happy to be back, especially in my "senior" years ... walking to the shapes, restaurants, the movie theatre ... .it is the perfect place to live. I'm glad I had the opportunity to live in other areas of Jacksonville, making lifelong friends, but this has been the best decision .... returning home to SAN MARCO.

Vicki Zambetti Coward – San Marco memories from 1940"s and early 1950s

Starting at the north end of San Marco Blvd. before there was Prudential and Baptist hospital, was an open lot where my father and his friends had baseball games on Sunday, this lot then became Mr. Fernety's golf driving range and later Baptist Hospital.

A couple of blocks south was the Texas Drive Inn. It is

a part of every young person's life that lived in the area.

The small park at the corner of San Marco and Landon was the daily gathering place for the toddlers.

Every Sat. morning we went to the San Marco Theater. We were treated to a double feature, plus a Newsreel, a cartoon, and a serial which always ended with an "about to happen" tragedy. You had to return the next week to get the resolution to that tragedy and begin a new one. By the way, we could only buy popcorn and a few candy bars. There was only a single water fountain, but admission was 9 cents.

On the same block were two grocery stores, Winn Lovett and Setzer's. In between were three notable establishments, The Town Pump, Mim's Bakery and A B Williams Drug Store. The first being the local bar and the second a very popular lunch spot. Mim's had a signature sandwich, cream cheese and nuts on their homemade toasted raisin bread. We sat at a U shaped counter. A B Williams was the time typical black and white tile drug store. One of the best features was in the front, the magazine section, especially the movie magazines, Photoplay" and "Modern Screen". This was our source for Hollywood gossip since there was no television.

Across Carlo Street was Kress's 5 and 10 cent store, which was really a miniature department store, and the Arcade Men's Shop. The Little Theater was already popular, directed by Paul Geisenhof. He was also the owner of the gift shop next to the fire station. The store operated for 40 years.

There was a curved building that housed the A&P Supermarket, Lane's drugstore and the bowling alley. Lane's was a favorite after school spot. The French fries were the best. This property is now the Bank of America.

Where the park now stands was a Gulf Filling Station. The fire station was working, flanked by Geisenhof's, Herman Jackson's cleaners, a beauty parlor, and Al's Men's Shop. Geisenhof's was previously occupied by the Tune Spot, our favorite record shop. My grandfather spent so much time visiting the fire station that the fire truck lead his funeral procession from the church to Oaklawn Cemetery.

The sidewalk in front of the theater was the very social bus stop. School age children could buy bus tokens for 4 cents which also entitled you to transfers so the bus was popular transportation.

All in all it was the best place anyone could want for a neighborhood.

LeAnna Cumber – San Marco became home in January 2011. This was a very significant year in my life— it included the birth of our son Jake and moving to Florida. Our move into the neighborhood was entirely unplanned and immensely lucky. We did not know it at the time, but had my family been able to take its time to look for a Jacksonville home we would have chosen San Marco. However, we did not have much time at all. Our move from Washington, DC was happening quickly so we had only 36 hours to find a home so that we would be settled in by the time Jake was born. Our house was the last one we looked at during this whirlwind house hunting experience. We fell in love immediately with the home, but, more importantly, with the neighborhood. People walking on every street, the huge trees with Spanish moss dangling, the historic homes, the Square and the beautiful parks. I closed my eyes and saw my family being happy in San Marco. What I did not know at the time was just how welcoming our neighbors would be and how much San Marco would feel like a small town in a big city. And it started with an invitation to the neighborhood Easter Egg hunt my then three-week old son attended.

I did not grow up in Jacksonville like many San Marco residents. My childhood home is Ann Arbor, Michigan. A place where as a child I walked and biked to school, friends' homes, parks, shops and restaurants. We knew our neighbors, they knew us, and I grew up with a strong sense of community. When we began our family I knew I wanted my children to grow up with that same sense of community, which can be challenging to find in an age of constant movement. Living in San Marco has allowed us to provide this environment to our two children (my daughter Poppy arrived in 2013).

The friendliness of the neighbors was on full display soon after we moved into our house. Within weeks of settling in, neighbors knocked on our door to introduce themselves, deliver baby gifts, bring over dinner right after Jake was born, invite us to Easter Egg hunts, and encourage us to get involved. Having lived in very large cities before, I was unprepared and incredibly touched and excited by the community's sense of family. In fact, nearly everyone we now know in Jacksonville has a direct connection to a San Marco neighbor or friend.

I was thrilled to have landed in such an amazing neighborhood and wanted to waste no time in getting involved. I attended my first San Marco Preservation Society (SMPS) meeting 5 weeks after Jake was born. I was hooked. It was so exciting to see my neighbors care so much about the small things like making sure small businesses thrived and that street lights were working and parks were thriving so kids could play safely. I am excited by the prospect of shaping my children's neighborhood and green spaces knowing that future young families will move into San Marco because of these qualities. I knew SMPS was a way to get involved and to add my voice and time behind the generations of leaders who made San Marco attractive to me. Today our children know everyone from our neighbors to the local policeman to the owner of the local toy store. They play in the parks, visit with the firemen, and ask to walk to ice cream and dinner. They are growing up with a strong sense of neighborhood identity and pride.

While I may have started out as an accidental San Marco resident, I and my family are thrilled to have become a permanent part of the San Marco community.

Mike Darragh – San Marco - A great date night and much more…

My wife and I moved to Jacksonville three times during my career. The third time, we settled in San Marco, drawn by the great elementary school, the hub of activity in San Marco, and the variety of people in the neighborhood. But we slowly realized that if we didn't plan a "date night" once every month or two, we wouldn't get any time to ourselves.

I'm not sure how we found Theatre Jacksonville. We had supported various arts organizations around town, but when we visited Theatre Jacksonville, we found people who really <u>wanted</u> us to enjoy ourselves. Sometimes arts professionals can seem a bit jaded while playing yet another gig; at Theatre Jacksonville we sensed that each person had

66

tried hard to get the role, and was doing everything possible to make the character come alive.

So, with a four-year-old and a one-year-old, in 1990 we committed to finding a babysitter five or six times each year, and we started attending every show. Each season we kept renewing, feeling like it was the best date night we could ask for.

It took over two decades before I discovered the secrets to the theater's magic. In 2011, when I was asked to join the theater's Board, I asked why we didn't double or triple prices so that we were closer to the cost of other entertainment. As I learned the answer over the next few months, I realized why Nancy and I had been so enamored with the productions.

Theatre Jacksonville is a <u>Community</u> Theater. That means that volunteer actors from the community audition to fill the roles—giving professionals and amateurs, alike, a chance to perform and hone their skills. It offers both fun fare (musicals and comedies) and thought-provoking dramas to enrich the quality of experience to the audience. It also uses its historic facility and its staff and volunteers to offer numerous other educational opportunities to the community. And it does all of this at a cost that allows virtually anyone in the community to take part.

Eventually, our kids grew up. They started going to the Theatre with us, and caught the bug. One wrote plays and got involved in the film industry. The other tried the stage in high school, then got to expand his skills with a mix of professionals and amateurs on Theatre Jacksonville's stage. He went on to college, landing a number of lead roles in his freshman year.

We continue to go to Theatre Jacksonville. Our kids are no longer at home, so we use "date night" now to go out to dinner with friends, see a show, and discuss it during intermission and afterwards—often as we stroll home. I guess we could stop going, turn on a comfortable cable channel, text each other as we watch, and live in our own, private world. But community isn't built while texting, or while staring at a TV screen. And, to me, life isn't as rich without community.

Andrew Dickson – When I moved to Jacksonville eighteen years ago to teach, I had no idea my real school would be my neighborhood. San Marco has educated me in the values of community.

As a young man, my first apartment on River Road taught me to attend sunset on the dock every day, and never take climate control for granted. The window unit just didn't cut the heat, and the vintage gas heater looked like it might blow sky-high. It was the hottest summer and coldest winter of my life, but it kept me in the company of neighbors with central heat & air.

But renting fosters only temporary relationships as people move on, and at the time I was expecting to move on myself. Fortunately, I did not. Instead, I met my bride. As a young husband, our first house on River Oaks Road taught me the importance of committing to a place. A few years later when our son was born, our neighbors finally introduced themselves. They knew the signs, and saw we were sticking around for a while.

Our next community was the dog walkers in FEC Park, where your dog's name and reputation preceded your own.

Living with dogs compresses life's events; they age and pass faster than we do, and so the dog walkers become supports for loss and celebrators of new arrivals. The dog park teaches lessons in compassion.

It turned out one of our dog walker friends ran a Montessori school just down the street from a house we had our eyes on. We bought the house when our daughter arrived. Many years after our children attended pre-school there, we still get waves and hugs when we walk by. My wife counts the Montessori Moms as some of her finest friends.

Before long, San Marco taught me leadership, when a development down the street threatened to turn our street into a busy thoroughfare. That experience led an invitation to work on San Marco by Design, and a 6-year stint at San Marco Preservation Society, reporting graffiti, saving the Balis Community Center from the budgetary chopping block, and improving Brown Whatley Park. Working for San Marco has given me a rolling tutorial in urban planning and community service, and has introduced me to many gracious mentors and neighbors. My children complain we can't take ten steps in the square without stopping to talk with somebody, but that's my idea of a community.

So, while I realize eighteen years is only a fraction of San Marco's history, those years and this place have shaped me as a teacher, husband, father, and activist. I'm grateful to San Marco for those lessons.

Malinda Dixon Durham – I am a child of San Marco, Hendricks Avenue Elementary, and Landon High School.

Why else would I return to Jacksonville after 40 years, to the south side of the river, to San Marco? Its home…

As I remember, Jacksonville in the 40's and 50's was like 3 distinct little towns, Southside, Riverside, and Springfield. There was Mandarin, of course, and the beach, and Orange Park and Lackawanna, but they were day-trips away. We had friends and family members in all directions but the rivalries among the three, particularly in high school athletics, were fierce.

Landon, Lee, and Jackson were all members of the Florida High School Athletics Association's "Big Ten", the most prestigious of all the conferences. We played our inter-city football games in the Gator Bowl, huge crowds of us caravanning from San Marco, across the River to the stadium. Fall Friday nights were the stuff movies are made of. (A self-proclaimed philosopher once said, "When the South lost the Civil War, they went to playin' football", and I believe it to be true.) Bands representing the 3 schools engaged in heated rivalries, too, and the student bodies, and the cheerleaders, and the parents. Landon was always competitive. In 1956, we were Big Ten Champs in football and co-Big Ten Champs in basketball.

George Wood was the principal of Landon at that time, a fine man and a true educator. Mike Houser, bless his heart, was Assistant Principal and Dean of Boys, beloved, even though the "boys" thought he wielded a mean paddle. Orra Eastburn was Dean of Girls and someone you never wanted to disappoint. Landon was blessed with an outstanding faculty and staff. Among them were Miss Nelly B. Kelly who taught Algebra, "Aunt" Ranna Smith, Junior English, and Hunter Perkins, Senior English. They were excellent teachers with fine reputations and they inspired us. And there was our legendary football coach, Barney "The Bear" Searcy. My recollection is that he "taught" 6 hours of study hall and ended each school day coaching the football team. The proof is in the pudding…

And then there were the Lionettes, the girls' drill team directed by Miss Kathleen Turner. Amazingly, when the Lionettes stood in single file, they stretched from one end of the Gator Bowl to the other. Practices were held every day, rain or shine, in the field behind the Southside Public Library. And Miss Turner, as so many Lionettes will attest, had the ability to get the most out of us. In addition to performing at half-time for Landon football teams' home games, the Lionettes were invited to perform at many inaugural events, holiday parades, and Bowl games. For one such game, the Meninak Bowl in Chattanooga, we ordered pencils to sell, embossed with "Landon Lions" to help finance our trip. Instead of "Landon Lions" they were embossed "Landon Loins". We sold them anyway.

As much a community happening as the Friday night football games were, so too was Thursday night at Dixon (no relation, just a good friend) Electric Company on the Square, for the weekly episodes of The Long Ranger. Before everyone had a set, Bob Dixon set up folding chairs among the refrigerator, washing machines, and radio displays for anyone and everyone to share in the miracle of television. There were never enough chairs.

On most Saturday mornings, Southside adolescents and teen-agers could be found at the San Marco Theater for the serial and the cowboy movie. Typically, there would be a row of young girls with a row of young boys behind them, (the 7th and 8th grade sets), and "couples" would be holding hands over the theater seats. I don't think my mother knew that. Nevertheless, many a serious romance got started to the crack of Lash LaRue's whip. Sometimes, smaller groups of those same adolescent and teen-age types would meet in the Square on Saturday morning, walk down Hendricks to the Main Street Bridge, cross it, make their way to Forsyth Street to buy a couple of 9c hamburgers and a coke at Krystal, and continue on to the Florida Theater for the matinee. Then they walked home. They walked! Just imagine.

The Square drew Landon students every day after school, walking home, looking for a ride, or catching the city bus which ran out Hendricks Avenue and San Jose to the neighborhoods which fed into Landon. We stood in long lines at the Rexall Drug Store for a banana split or a cherry coke, or walked across the street to the bakery to purchase and share a dozen fresh-baked Parker House Rolls. Sometimes we did both. When we finally started driving, we drove to The Texas for a bar-b-que sandwich and a limeade and a little "cruising". It was at The Texas that I smoked for the first time,--a Viceroy, of course. My mother never knew that, either. Neither did Miss Eastburn.

It was in the early 50's that Prudential Insurance Company moved many families from New Jersey to Jacksonville to open their new offices. Because of the high regard so many had for San Marco, its retail and its neighborhoods, and the strength of the schools in the area, many of them located in these neighborhoods. They were welcomed into the community as newcomers are today, their children quickly assimilated into the schools, and many of these families are represented in San Marco today.

So, being a child of San Marco, of Hendricks Avenue Elementary, and Landon High School, my grandchildren are trained to say as they cross the river and before the San Marco exit, "This is the St. Johns and it flows north". And, "This is San Marco and Landon High School is right over there". And, finally, "That's Hendricks Avenue Elementary School where Minda never lost a foot race". My hope for them is that they are making memories, good ones, and that someday they will know when they are home.

Brian Doyle – Gate River Run

Gate River Run is one of the great annual events in the city of Jacksonville. The Jacksonville Track Club formed it more than 40 years ago. The event has grown astronomically over the years, now hosting more than 25,000 runners from all over the United States. The event is a 15-kilometer race, which is equal to 9.3 miles. San Marco has been fortunate enough to be an important part of this special event for a long time. As the runners come off the main street bridge they head down San Marco Boulevard. They then take a right onto River Road and have a great view of the river from River Front Park. The run then from mile two to mile five winds though our great neighborhood. The route runs down River Road to River Oaks Road, then heads back up Hendricks before taking a right on South Alexandria and Belote before turning on Atlantic and crossing the train tracks heading out of San Marco. The event is one that many San Marco residents not only cheer on friends and family, but also participate in. The race is the perfect distance for anyone thinking of doing something challenging, but rewarding. As a lifelong Jacksonville resident I can remember getting up early on that second Saturday in March every year as a child and heading over to my Aunt and Uncles house on River Road right about the 3.5 mile mark. We would stand in their front yard and wait for the runners to come by. As they started running by you thought they would never stop coming. Every once in a while I would hear one of my family members shout at someone who ran by and cheer him or her on. That is the great thing about this event. It is an event for everyone. Anyone can do it. Whether you train or not you should definitely experience the Gate River Run at least once.

Kiley Efron – My husband Chef Sam Efron and I opened our restaurant Taverna, in San Marco 7 years ago. Prior to that the space was occupied by a local favorite restaurant Café Carmon, for over 20 years. We moved to Jacksonville 10 years ago from San Francisco. My husband was born and raised in Jacksonville, and we were excited to be a part of what we considered to be an emerging food scene, ripe with potential. We knew that Jacksonville would be a great place to build a business and a family. The only question was what part of Jacksonville we wanted to call home professionally and personally. Having been born in raised in California I was immediately drawn to the historic charm and beauty of San Marco. Beauty and Charm aside we knew the location would attract people from all over the city and the combination of diverse shops, beautiful scenery, and incredible residential neighborhood surrounding it would make for the perfect place to start a business and raise our family. Instincts proved right and we have lived and worked in San Marco area ever since.

The part we love most about owning a business in this neighborhood is the incredible sense of community there is between our fellow business neighbors and the residents who are devoted to supporting the businesses within it. We love seeing the same people out playing with their kids in the park, walking their dogs, grabbing a cup of coffee, shopping at their favorite San Marco Boutiques and drinking wine on our patio. Many of our guests live in the neighborhood, they bring their kids in for family dinners, celebrate graduations, birthdays and date nights with us. Like them we have chosen to raise our kids in this beautiful community and feel so blessed to be a part of it.

Val Feinberg Evans – Celebrations elicit introspection and reminiscing. As I think about San Marco, the neighborhood we choose to raise a family, and now the place I call home upon celebrating our twentieth year this past March 2016. This year we also celebrated our first son, Jesse, graduating from high school and now beginning college while our second son, Austin, entered his senior year of high school. We have celebrated many milestones as a family. We have shared special occasions with our neighbors and participated in the many annual events hosted in this very special place we call home.

When we relocated to Jacksonville in 1996, I spent most of the first two months exploring the city driving north to south and east to west. I observed the varied communities and researched Jacksonville's history with a particular interest in the historic neighborhoods close to the Downtown. When I read about San Marco it intrigued me. When I discovered San Marco Square, with the quaint shops and lovely homes with views of the St. Johns, I knew it was the place I wanted my children to grow up. I remember driving up and down streets looking for home sale signs.

I was determined to find a modest home within walking distance to schools and parks. We looked at homes that were beyond our budget, homes that were in need of major renovations, homes that were too small, homes that were not our taste. We also found a home that with a little paint and some imagination became our home. We found the perfect street with wonderful neighbors. It is a mile from Hendricks Avenue Elementary School and a ¼ mile from Granada Park with big, beautiful Oak trees (that have provided us with many a story). We found a small town in the midst of a large city.

I love the perspective of San Marco when I meander around on foot or by bicycle. Sometimes stopping at the park to sit on a swing remembering my boys running around with the other kids and sharing the trials and tribulations of life with other moms and dads. We have watched our children as the city and our small town continued to evolve and change mostly in a good way. And sometimes we were challenged as a neighborhood to preserve our quality of life and we did and our children watched and learned and became immersed in all that is San Marco.

I stand at the base of the lion's fountain in the square and find the bricks with names of our children. Twenty years ago the square looked a bit different, but it still embodies all the qualities that make it a great place.

Christopher D Flagg, FASLA – The San Marco Preservation Society (SMPS) embarked upon a process to preserve and enhance the vitality of the community's economic and social values, its health and charm, combined with improving its transportation and street "sense" and historical context. This "action plan" ultimately became the guiding framework for Smart Growth principals providing strategic decision making regarding the evolution of the physical environment, the accommodation of changing market conditions and identifying the context for which this community can grow.

When this effort was contemplated, it was determined not to create just another "plan" for the neighborhood; rather, it became an opportunity to reflect on the values for which San Marco offered its stakeholders. It was a time to reflect upon an ideal image for the community and how best to approach a process to ensure that its character is sustained for future generations.

This process was a culmination of past efforts combined with an infusion of current stakeholder dialogue to recognize and promote future infill development which would ultimately make the most economic and aesthetic sense for the community as a whole. It also presented an opportunity to explore multiple facets of sustainability, such as the connection between health and the built environment combined with safe and walkable streets, bikeways, traffic calming and low impact development principals.

The early and often engagement of community stakeholders, business owners, residents and politicians, opened the creative doors of contextual innovation, keeping the character and scale of the neighborhoods in mind while still exploring the benefits of future economic development drivers. This strategy for planning was determined to be a successful Smart Growth plan which defined place within the natural and build environment, its unique history and its political and social community structure.

A successful approach usually leads to successful results. By being highly interactive and inclusive, the plan has become a valuable tool in San Marco's long term growth planning.   Growth initiatives must be flexible and technologically savvy, while still adhering to the qualities of its character and history. A quick summary of the process was as follows:

- The review of existing neighborhood conditions
- Objectives were discussed and vetted publically through multiple "topical" workshops
- "Place" was defined
- An "Action Plan" was devised and recommended
- Future considerations were developed

San Marco by Design: A Smart Growth Plan for North San Marco now serves as corollary guidance to the City of Jacksonville Planning and Development Department for creating a Special District Code or Form-Based Code for San Marco and other neighborhoods.

George Foote – I moved to San Marco in the late 80's when the neighborhood was in a bit of transition. That said, I felt it was the best place to be for my small but growing family. Work brought us to Jacksonville in 1984 and my wife, Michele, and I initially lived in an apartment on the river in Arlington and then built a home in Mandarin in 1985. Both of those neighborhoods were fine in their own way, but we were drawn to San Marco for the small town feel, schools, churches, and beautiful homes. However, through my years as a resident of this community, I have learned that the residents of San Marco are a special group of people and the real reason San Marco is such a great place.

It's ironic that, in a community full of tradition, it was my own tradition that helped me find my home in San Marco. My college roommate, Tony Papas, and I make it a point to

attend the annual Florida vs. Georgia college football game...
a.k.a., The World's Largest Outdoor Cocktail Party, The
Border War, or known today as The Florida Georgia Football
Classic. We've carried out this tradition since 1979. Tony
hasn't missed a game in 36 years and I've only missed one.
Michele and I actually watched the game on TV from a cruise
ship docked in Alexandria, Egypt that year. But back to our
story... Tony and I were headed down Hendricks Avenue on
our way to the 1987 edition of the game when I saw the "For
Sale by Owner" sign on Berwick Road. The two story red-
brick home looked like the perfect place. Michele and I visited
with the owners the next day, put down our deposit on the spot,
and in January 1988 we officially became residents of the San
Marco community.

Our son Joseph was 2 years old that month and our son
Garrett was born in the fall of that year. Their sister Regan
came along 10 years later, and as I'm writing this, our
grandson, Cassius James Foote, has just arrived (San Marco's
newest resident). Congratulations to Brittney and Garrett!

As a family, we have tried to soak up all that San
Marco has to offer. Visiting the San Marco branch of the
Jacksonville Library was a weekly event when the children
were young and playing the many parks was an important part
of our routine. We have enjoyed worshiping and serving at
Southside Baptist Church, playing baseball at HAB, and going
on excellent adventures with the local Boy & Girl Scout troops.
Regan also spent 15 years at Studio K Dance and Studio
owner, Niki Stokes, let me pick the theme of the Dad Dance in
Regan's last year. We got to bring Star Wars to the stage and I
gained a perfect excuse to buy some Jedi Knight robes.

Some of my favorite memories include seeing my son, Garrett, load his 12 foot sailboat on a wagon, pull it down though River Oaks Park and sail it into the St. Johns river with his friends. My son Joseph stole home to win the game against a rival at HAB that was known for that very same skill. He "Stanfielded" the Stanfields that day and I'll never forget it.

I'm grateful for the many friends and families that we have come to know in our time here in San Marco and thankful for their friendship. Michele and I also want to thank all the neighbors, teachers, leaders, and coaches that have invested in our children through the years. You have been a blessing and we appreciate you more than you know.

Maureen Foster – I moved to San Marco 5 years ago and I absolutely love it here. I am fortunate enough to live close to both the Square and the River, I try to walk to either one of them at least 4 times a week.

I love taking photos of the sunsets and other niche areas in our little community, albeit by an iPhone, just snaps along the way of my walks or bike rides.

I have always wanted to live in San Marco, since the moment that I saw The Rocky Horror Picture Show at the San Marco Theater, back in the mid 80's. I made it happen 5 years ago and now my son and his wife bought their first home off of Hendricks and are official "San Marconites".

The ambiance of the square with those lions being our land mark is so charming and now we are welcoming more small businesses and restaurants, which is going to grow our little community in a great way!!

Whether I'm picking up coffee at Starbucks early in the morning or stopping by The Grotto or The Grape and Grain for a glass of wine in the evening, I always think to myself, how lucky am I to live in such a wonderful community.

Now....about that Publix coming soon...ha-ha!!

Happy 90th Birthday San Marco... here's to many-many more!!

Cindy Graves – In the late 1990's, Southside Baptist Church created a Christmas display that has become a beloved San Marco tradition. In conjunction with the church's musical presentation of The Singing Christmas Tree, members loaned their personal manger scenes to be displayed in the prayer chapel as a reminder that the birth of Christ – God's gift of His Son to the world – is the real reason for the celebration of Christmas.

No Room at the Inn has grown over the years to include over one hundred different nativity sets from dozens of countries, many of which are handmade. They range in dimension from one tiny enough to fit in a matchbox, to figures that are almost life-size. The centerpiece of the display is a miniature re-creation of the village of Bethlehem, featuring over 25 lighted buildings and more than 300 figures and animals. The nativities are made of an amazing variety of materials, from traditional porcelain or plaster-of-paris, to ebony and other woods, fabric, stone, corn husks … even soda cans and recycled auto parts.

Many of the nativities reflect the countries or cultures from which they originate. There is an African nativity that features a zebra and giraffe instead of the traditional cow and donkey; a set from Laos that depicts the stable built on stilts and Jesus lying in a cradle swinging from the rafters; a Louisiana crèche with a chef, a jazz musician and a Choctaw chief as the wise men. There is even a set with wise <u>women</u>! The artisans who craft the "traditional" cast of nativity characters with their own ethnic features and costumes reinforce the biblical truths that Christ came for the whole world, and that He dwells in the heart of all who will let Him in.

Because Southside Baptist wants this to be truly a community event, for several years *No Room at the Inn* has moved out of the church and into San Marco, sometimes displayed in empty stores on the Square and sometimes sharing space with generous retailers, such as Woodside Lane or Stellers Art Gallery. This allows many more people to enjoy the beauty of the nativities and to be reminded of the message of Christmas. It also encourages other community residents to offer their crèches for display or even to create their own, including the young man who for several years shared his original Lego nativities!

No Room at the Inn is a labor of love ... a gift offered by Southside Baptist Church to the community that lies within the shadow of its steeple, and a tangible reminder of the hope that Christmas brings of "peace on earth, good will to men."

Stephanie & Willow Grau – When I asked my six year old daughter what she loves most about living in our neighborhood, she responded without hesitation: "Seeing our neighbors." Upon consideration, I couldn't agree more. On the surface, San Marco has a lot to offer: restaurants, boutique shops, playgrounds and parks, not to mention the beautiful homes and neighborhoods that are unique to this zip code. But what really make this neighborhood special are the neighbors.

We bought our home during our first year of marriage nearly ten years ago, intending for it to be our "starter" home. Since that time, we have welcomed two lovely children into our family, but our little family has more than doubled, as we have been blessed to find family in our neighbors as well. Wonderful neighbors are something that cannot be bought, and they add inestimable value to our property.

In case anyone is curious, my six year old's second favorite thing about our neighborhood is Peterbrooke's chocolate covered popcorn. I'll second that one, too.

Quinn Johnston Gray, 5th grade – Hendricks Avenue Elementary is the best elementary school in San Marco. I love our school because it feels like home. I feel that way because everyone here is super nice and friendly. My teachers are kind of like aunts or uncles because they are helpful, kind, and they are not mean. My friends are like cousins because they are always nice and they play a lot.

Janet Hogshead – San Marco Holiday Home Tour

In October, 1975, the newly formed San Marco Preservation Society was looking for ways to support needed projects in the community. The suggested idea of a Home Tour seemed perfect for our historic and beautiful San Marco.

Though many historic homes were offered, the first Tour included: The Robert Barnes residence at 1950 Largo Place, the Bryan Dowling residence at 832 Sorrento Road, the Harold Catlin residence at 1971 River Road, the Howard Hogshead residence at 2103 River Road and the Earl Hadlow residence at 2171 River Road, all houses built in the 1920s and 30s on the original plats.

So many people were eager to help. Wade Hampton was General Chairman aided by Ward Lariscy and Pat Barnes. Others included Larry Wilson, Ginny Stine, Peg Alcorn, Forrest Brewer, Celeste Hampton, Lee Mercier, Muff Whatley Law and John Currington. Each room of the Tour Houses had a docent eager to tell the history of the house. Not only did people from San Marco come, but from all parts of the city! It was an entertaining and financial success.

In the following years, more variety was added, including our historic Firehouse, the relocated Carpenter Gothic church on Belote Green, a lighted Christmas tree floating on a barge in Lake Marco, musicians playing in every home, and refreshments at the River Road median, Davin Park. Often the Tour coincided with other activities, and the whole area was alive with the clip-clop of horse-drawn carriages, the Living Nativity, music in the Square, and lit by area-wide luminaria. Carolers and neighbors were out and about, greeting each other in the Christmas spirit. A wonderful memory of life in San Marco!

Nancy Hogshead – We moved to San Marco in 1973 when I was eleven and just going into sixth grade. We loved our new house, but there surely was a lot of grass for me and my brother Andy to mow.

Our next door neighbors were Wade and Celeste Hampton, who were very involved with the Jacksonville community, and particularly with San Marco. The Hamptons helped our family get acquainted with the city. Because they were so loving and supportive to our family, and particularly to me, I choose them for my Godparents, a warm relationship I cherish to this day.

The day we moved in, I began swimming on the Randy Reese Swim Team. By 1980, I'd broken American and world records, competed all over the world and won a place on the USA Olympic Team. Unfortunately, the Soviet Union invaded Afghanistan, and the U.S. team, along with most of our western allies, did not compete in the Moscow Olympics.

I gave up on my Olympic dreams. I did go to Duke on a full athletic scholarship; the school's first. However, I had no role models of women who were still elite swimmers at the old age of 22; Title IX was just starting to have these far-reaching effects.

But like letting go of a ball, my Olympic dream bounced back into my hand and my heart after a few years. Half-way through my junior year, I took a leave of absence from Duke to train harder than I'd ever trained. I made the 1984 Olympic team in five events.

I'd been dreaming about competing in the Olympics for more than half of my short life, and I have to say that the reality was even bigger than I could have possibly imagined. The streets of Los Angeles were all decorated with banners and the city was whole-heartedly welcoming. My family was all there cheering for me. The police took a look at my badge and were ready to take me anywhere with the lights flashing.

The first event at the 1984 Olympics was the 100 meter freestyle, my event. And I Won! In a Tie! With fellow American teammate and roommate! For the first time ever, two gold medals were awarded for the same event; two Americans in an Olympics held in America. There's a picture of me in the New York Times with my slack-jaw expression; seeing the same time for both of us on the scoreboard. Best of all, I won my first Gold Medal on Celeste Hampton's birthday. There were two more gold medals and a silver to come.

San Marco welcomed me on my return. There were billboards and hundreds of telegrams and letters. Someone put a sign in our yard "HOME OF JACKSONVILLE'S GOLDEN GIRL" in red, white and blue, a Jacksonville celebration, where Mayor Jake Godbold gave me a key to the city and I signed cute kids' autographs for hours. It was wonderful to be back home in San Marco sharing Olympic memories with my family and friends. Thanks Jacksonville!

Chester Holland, **5th grade** – One of the things that makes San Marco special is my school. I like Hendricks Avenue Elementary because of all the friendships. Also, when I'm riding my bike to school, I know that when I go through the doors, I'm going to enter a world of learning and wonder. When I go inside the media center in the morning, I see the eager faces of the school broadcasters, ready to talk about the weather and sports. Last but not least, every day the minds of the teachers are ready to teach the minds of the future astronauts and engineers.

Sarah Marie Johnston – I'll never forget seeing San Marco for the first time. It was February 1999, and my boyfriend (future husband), Tom Gray, and I had just travelled across country from California in a rented diesel U-Haul truck with a car in-tow. The 55 MPH governor placed on the vehicle had made the trip extra slow, extra boring, and extra bumpy. After accidental delays going through Louisiana (neither of us knew it was Mardi Gras!), we finally hit the last long stretch of the Florida Panhandle and neared our destination of exit 350B, just after the I-10 / I-95 split.

As it has been many times over the years since then, the San Marco exit was under construction at the time, and our descent off the freeway was a bit precarious with the trailer bumping behind us as we navigated the tight turns from the construction barricades and tried to follow our map to guide us to the place we would soon call "home". We drove through the San Marco Square and I marveled at the quaintness of it, feeling somehow that I'd landed on a movie set. Driving down the road and taking the right at the "split" from Hendricks Avenue onto "Old San Jose", passing the Duck Pond, and then pulling into the driveway of our new little house will forever be as vividly etched in my memory as my wedding day.

While Tom knew it was a nice neighborhood (having grown up in Orange Park, not everything was as unknown to him as it was to me), we had gotten lucky to find a rental home, sight-unseen, in the Miramar Terrace neighborhood of San Marco. Learning that Tom, their future renter was a professional chef, the owners had undertaken a remodel of the home's kitchen and installed a new gas stove, refrigerator and other amenities, which we took as one of the first signs that we'd landed in the "right place!" Mind you, this was well before cell phones, Google Maps, and the volumes of encyclopedic knowledge available night or day to do research about neighborhoods, activities, real estate, or the like on the internet. We honestly couldn't have done any better if that all *had* existed. The little rental house was perfect, the neighbors were welcoming, and starting our new life in Jacksonville could not have been more ideal. Of course, we had no idea at that time, that San Marco would be the place that over the years we would build a successful business, purchase our first "starter" home, and later our "forever" home, have our son, Quinn, and become as intertwined in the fabric of the community as we have over the years.

Yet, that is all exactly what *has* happened, for us, and many like us (such as my mother, Judith, who relocated to San Marco from California in 2009) with similar stories of arriving here from wherever place, and whatever time, under whatever circumstance, and knowing instinctively they were "home". What has also become very clear, now looking back on the 18 years we have lived in San Marco, is that while technically, it is a pinpoint on a map (or GPS locator, or perhaps in the most modern parlance, a Pokéstop), it is so much more than that. It is a place where dreams are born and realized, where lifelong friendships are formed and nurtured, where the sound of kids playing in the park is as commonplace as hearing the bells of the nearest church peal out their Sunday morning melodies, and where we feel so lucky to be contributing members of the community that makes San Marco such a rich place, in the very best meaning of the word, to belong.

Tara Kendall – There are many things I appreciate about San Marco; the fact that it is an active community is one of my favorites. The streets can get downright crowded with bikers, runners, dog walkers, and families out for a leisurely stroll or bike ride. It never ceases to inspire me to lace up my shoes and get out of the house and join them.

I was born and raised in a charming brick house on a friendly street in San Marco in the 80's, and was lucky enough to attend the wonderful neighborhood schools. I attended Hendricks Avenue Elementary, Landon Middle School, and graduated from Wolfson High School. At Wolfson, I went out for the Cross Country team simply because I needed to participate in a sport and I was assured I would not be cut. I had no way of knowing then that this would foster a lifelong love of running and become an essential part of who I am, even though today it is more of a slow jog rather than a run.

Over the years I ventured out and lived in other parts of Jacksonville and St. Johns County; however, I never found an area where I enjoyed living and running as much as I did in the San Marco area. After graduating college, marriage, and having two amazing children I finally made my way back to the San Marco area. We bought a house in my old neighborhood and I was pleased to find the same friendly supportive running community I remembered from my adolescence.

Every day, no matter what time I run, I encounter other runners who are always ready to offer a kind greeting, a wave, a simple smile or even just a nod of their head. There are always people out in the calm silent morning at 5 am or well after dark. I have yet to complete a run without encountering another soul.

The streets feel safe, they offer plenty of shady spots and are well maintained. There are even many public water fountains dispersed on my routes which are so convenient. One of my favorite loops is to run from my home down to River Road and admire the majestic houses along the tree lined street.

There is a stretch at the end that offers unobstructed views of our beautiful river. It is quite a reward to catch it right at sunrise.

My family is excited to have returned to San Marco and I look forward to many more years running these familiar streets.

R. Ward Lariscy – In 1967 I started working at May Cohens Department Store downtown and found San Marco to be a convenient place to live and rented an apartment on San Marco Boulevard with a bus stop on the corner making it easy to reach work without driving. The neighborhood proved to be the ideal place to live with all the necessary shops within walking distance, grocery, movies, drug stores and restaurants. The A&P Grocery store in the square packaged meats in small amounts and butter could be bought by the stick and you didn't have to buy the package of four, even gladiolus for a dollar a bunch in the summer. I found the neighborhood was filled with many retired persons who had bought there when the neighborhood was new and there were few families with children. I started searching for a permanent home in the neighborhood and bought an "as is" house in 1971 with termites holding hands to keep the doors open. Not long after, the neighborhood started changing with more young families moving in as the original home owners died or moved out. The younger neighbors of San Marco joined together to form the San Marco Preservation and started the rebirth of the old neighborhood. We had a number of bicycle tours of the area with stops at locations and would inform the riders of the history of the stop. Yearly covered dish meals were held in the parks on holidays. In 1981 I opened my Interior Design business by renting in the Square on the North side that had formerly been American Import Lighting. Later moving the design business to Prudential Drive and turning the Square location into The Wardroom Ltd. for decorative accessories. The Square has seen many changes as the neighborhood changed. Lunch counters in drug stores and bakeries have now become gourmet restaurants and bars. New life has returned to the neighborhood.

Betty Lou Leuthold, 5ᵗʰ grade – Well, my mom owns a toy store in San Marco Square and my school is a-m-a-z-i-n-g. What's really great about San Marco is that it is a great community, has great kids, and no crime. Hendricks is such an easy simple school and I like that because through the years it's been like a super big house and everyone inside is family. All of the kids and teachers are such nice people and the fact that we get to stay there from kindergarten up till 5ᵗʰ grade is just so good I can't even find a word for it.

Jorge Lopez – Why I love my neighborhood- San Marco

My neighborhood is truly very special! Some of the wonderful things about my neighborhood include the gorgeous St John's river, majestic oak trees, great parks, delicious restaurants, exciting and fun events that take place throughout the year at the square, the spectacular architecture, the San Marco theatre, and some of the best schools around.

Although these attributes in and of itself make San Marco a great neighborhood, it is not the best reason for loving my neighborhood. The number 1 reason is because San Marco is like the Cheers Bar on the old "Cheers" TV show. Anywhere you go, especially at the square, just like "Cheers", everybody knows your name, and your kid's names, and sometimes even your parent's names. The community is so close that you can't go to Starbucks or Taverna or Pizza Palace or Beach Diner or Peterbrooke Chocolates (just to name a few) on any given day, without running into half of your friends from the neighborhood and spending an hour or 2 talking about things. And don't even think of going to a San Marco event without adding a couple of hours just to chat with all the friends you will run into. It is truly a community in every sense. It is an amazing community that truly cares and loves their community. That is what makes my neighborhood truly the best and why I love it!

Missie Sarra LePrell – San Marco is "home" to me in many different ways. When I moved here from New York City at the age of 13 I learned to love San Marco. Back then, the local bowling alley was the hangout for young people.

Today, I make my home on River Road, where my husband Sam and I live in a house that is quintessentially San Marco – with historic charm, but also with the necessary conveniences of modern times. The transformation of San Marco has followed the same pattern.

I see that transformation on a daily basis, because I spend much of my time helping other people make San Marco their home.

As a Realtor who works with residents to buy and sell their homes, I handle a lot of transactions in San Marco. While buyers care about the house or condominium, they care even more about the lifestyle of the neighborhood. San Marco offers a marvelous lifestyle for people at every step of their lives whether they are singles, couples, families, empty nesters, or seniors.

The heart of the area is San Marco Square, which features restaurants, shopping, boutiques, theater, movies, galleries & services that are convenient and enjoyable. Our neighborhood has St. Johns River access, numerous parks, a public library, a tennis complex, and, most importantly, some of the best schools in the city. We are convenient to Downtown, and have easy access to highways that connect San Marco to every part of Northeast Florida.

Through the work of the San Marco Preservation Society, those modern conveniences have not come at the expense of our unique historic character. San Marco is the perfect blend of the old and the new. We see that in our homes, which range from condominiums to two bedroom bungalows to grand waterfront estates. While these homes feature a variety of styles and tastes, they all maintain the historic feel for which San Marco is so well known.

When I show property to buyers from out of town and take them on a City tour, I always show them San Marco. No matter where they end up living—even if it is in the Beaches area—they remember San Marco and make it a "must go to stop" for dining & shopping throughout the year. Even more importantly, they see that San Marco is a neighborhood that encourages local gathering and walks through the parks, streets, and square.

Over the last several decades, our neighborhood has grown, changed, prospered, and fought efforts to undermine our unique character. San Marco will continue to improve without sacrificing the historic charm that has made it one of Florida's great neighborhoods. We may have struggles over how to maintain that balance, but San Marco residents have long proven their commitment to keeping our community special.

San Marco will always be the place that I call home -- and the neighborhood I want to help people buy and sell their own homes.

Eddie Lockamy – In 1954 the First Singing Christmas Tree was born in Charlotte North Carolina on the outside steps of a local funeral home. Known also as the Living Christmas Tree, this holiday tradition began in San Marco in the late-sixties. San Marco resident Sam Fillingham visited a Singing Christmas Tree in another city and came back to Jacksonville to build the first metal structure for Southside Baptist Church. The all-steel tree was fabricated and delivered in pieces for volunteers to assemble the second week-end of December. After a few years of holiday performances, the Singing Christmas tree was discontinued but brought back to life in 1986 as a San Marco tradition. Under the direction of Dr. Eddie Lockamy the Singing Christmas Tree was a yearly treat for thousands who came to witness one of four performances each year. The Tree had anywhere from 60 to 70 singers with many behind the scene volunteers who made each performance a heart-warming experience year after year. In addition to the music presented, there were guest artists, puppets, drama and soloists who added to each celebration. For many years the first presentation was unique in that it was presented to the homeless of Jacksonville. Residents of the shelters were transported each year for the first-night presentation. The show was preceded with a great Christmas feast and show and ended with gifts given to each guest. This San Marco tradition continued for 18 more years with a new repertoire of songs and guest artists each year. The memories of this Christmas tradition continue on in the lives of many Jacksonville residents and it made San Marco and Southside Baptist Church a favorite place to begin the Christmas season.

Mark MacLean – Several years ago, I had the honor and privilege of serving as the President of the San Marco Preservation Society, a tremendous organization that has done so much good over the years. An added benefit of being involved with the San Marco Preservation Society was having an opportunity to meet many of the people who have worked tirelessly for the benefit of the San Marco community over many years.

One of the first people I met in the San Marco community was a wonderful lady named Barbara Puckett. She immediately befriended me with a warmth and hospitality that became representative of San Marco for me. Barbara was part steel magnolia, part traditional Southern belle, mixed with modernity and style. She bridged all those elements together perfectly. Many of those who knew her as well would agree with me. In a way, as I think back on my friend Barbara, I believe she personified the best of San Marco; bridging the best of the past with a vision towards the future and incorporating both of those aspects into something new, unique and better. So when I think of San Marco, tradition and heritage are important, but incorporating those into a new, vibrant mix is important as well. Like many other neighborhoods, San Marco has, in its history, gone through various cycles of prosperity and decline. However unlike many other neighborhoods, San Marco had a treasure of history and tradition to be relied upon, to be preserved, restored and, in some cases, remade into something completely new; reflective of the past, but revived and keeping pace and boldly moving into the future.

When I look at the Lions fountain in the square, I see something relatively new to the San Marco community, yet representative of the tradition out of which the neighborhood came into being. A bit of the beautiful and ancient Saint Mark's square of Venice, brought here and made into what is now an iconic symbol of the Square and of the entire San Marco community. The same holds true for the monument at the northern end of the Square, the Balis Park gazebo, the new pedestrian lawn nearby, while the Theatre Jacksonville building and the San Marco Theater testify to San Marco's timeless style. A community and place that is a marvelous bridge between the past, present and future - it is San Marco.

Karen McCombs – In the spring of 1994, my husband Buddy accepted a new position with (then) Alliance Mortgage so we faced a big move from Falls Church, Va. Our children were 15 and 13 and our timeline was short. We had one week to figure out schools and one week to find a house. After deciding on Bishop Kenny for Scott and Episcopal for Jamie all we needed was a place to live. As you might imagine this is was a very emotional move for the kids and after visiting schools and driving around to get our bearings I felt an ice cream sundae was in order. We found ourselves in the Square in San Marco sitting outside under an umbrella trying to get a grip on our new reality when Scott looked at me and said (in a very serious tone) "I don't know about this place Mom, it seems a lot like Mayberry."

Well, enough said. There were probably only 4 houses on the market and only one in our price range. We offered full price (silly northerners) and ended up on Holly Lane. We are pretty sure luck was on our side because we bought a great house and the kids finished high school and college.

Coming from a very close knit neighborhood in Falls Church our expectations were big, and we were not disappointed. I have made wonderful friends in the community and have enjoyed being involved in the Preservation Society as well as a number of other organizations. Our friends come to visit and we see what we have through their eyes and we hope we never take our neighborhood for granted. It is a very special place. If you need proof, just look at all the new communities being developed. They would love to have what we have.

John McCoy – I worked off and on at the Day N Nite/Huntley Jiffy/Lil Champ on the corner of Hendricks & LaSalle since the early 70's. Got an autographed picture when Barbara Eden stayed at a B&B on River Rd. behind the old Sherwoods/Wormans. Got it in the 80s. River Phoenix and his band played the Bad Boy Club. When President Clinton was in town and he jogged on River Rd. along San Marco Beach. Almost every band and touring artist washed their clothes at the Kleene Place laundromat next to my store.

Diane Martin – It was 1997 when Tim and I moved to San Marco. I knew very few people there because I had recently moved to town, and worked out of my home office and traveled almost every week.

In the fall of 2005, I volunteered to Co-Chair the Patron's Party with Karen McCombs, met a lot of new friends, and really enjoyed it. Next thing you know, I was asked to join the Board of San Marco Preservation as the Events Chair.

I had a list of things I wanted to do: make the Concert in the Park better; start a 5k Fun Run; have movies in the park; a rescue dog event; continue the successful Rain Gutter Regatta...and I thought I could do it all.

Before I came on board, the Concert in the Park was a very small event, and I remember the bands were free. So I scheduled them twice a year, once in May and again in October, before the time changed. The first band I hired was Noel Friedline, and we had a great turnout. Over the next 6-7 years, I hired many good bands, from the Boogie Freaks, to Cloud 9, to the Navy Band! At some point, we started offering reserved tables to raise funds to pay for the bands. We also offered wood-fired pizza and other food-truck fare for those who didn't bring a picnic. We even sold beer and wine. It became THE event for the neighborhood and filled the park with friends and neighbors, kids and dogs!

I also organized the Bark in the Park to raise awareness for animals that needed a good home. There was a performance by the Frisbee dogs, a demonstration by the K-9 police dogs, and lots of rescue dogs and cats up for adoption. There was a competition for best pet tricks and best costume. We even crowned a Mr. and Miss San Barco! The first year, the judges were two San Marco ladies who were in a runoff to be an actual Judge!

I never got to have a 5k Fun Run, or have movies in the park, but I enjoyed putting on all those other events. I knew that other neighborhoods didn't do them, and things like this helped give San Marco its charm.

Richard Moore – My Life in San Marco

I have lived the majority of my life in San Marco and frankly can't imagine living anywhere else. Born in San Jose Forest, my parents, myself, and my baby brother moved to Oriental Gardens in 1971 into a new house next door to where my mother had lived for 11 years prior to marrying my father. I spent the next 10 years playing in the neighborhood, marveling at the swans living in the pond across the street, catching frogs and snakes in the other ponds hidden in plain sight, never knowing that Oriental Gardens was actually just that; a tourist attraction of natural springs and gardens that had now become the home of my youth.

After a small detour to central and south Florida for some book learning , my new wife Deborah (a south Florida native), returned to apartment living in Jacksonville and began our search for a more permanent home. Although our first choice was my childhood neighborhood, we had trouble finding something we both loved and could afford so our search expanded to other parts of town, much to my chagrin. However, our fortunes changed one day when Deborah called and said she had found something in San Marco. I immediately drove by and thought she had lost her mind, but 2 days later we were the owners of a house in San Marco. Twenty six years later, with our 16 year old son Trey, we still live in the same house, just down the street from where I grew up and where my parents still live.

I sometimes force my son to listen to the stories of my youth, like riding my bike to Peterson's in the square to buy sling shots and BB's (don't ask what we did with them) or hanging out playing pinball and eating burgers in the greasy spoon that would become the Metro Diner. I have seen San Marco change, but, for the most part, it has remained the same inviting neighborhood that I remember so fondly. When I was asked to serve on the Board of the San Marco Preservation Society, later becoming the President, my life in San Marco had come full circle and it was an honor.

This holiday season, my family will gather at my house or at my parent's house in San Marco, and we will celebrate yet another year in the neighborhood. I hope that my son and nieces and nephews remember San Marco as fondly as I do when they get old like me.

Tom Morris – Whether it is the soft whops of volleying at the Southside Park Complex   tennis courts on Hendricks Avenue, the constant patter of feet during the River Run, ultimate Frisbee play in FEC Park, fishing off the River Road bulkhead, the San Marco area variety of sports activities.

One sport that was not as obvious when my wife and I moved into the area in 1976 was the youth baseball fields behind the Hendricks Avenue Baptist Church. They are now more visible with the removal of buildings on Hendricks for the construction of a Daily's Station.

Two of the fields were built in the late 1940s thanks to the generosity of a church member who donated the land to the church on condition they be used for athletics. At that time, the church had teams that played other leagues throughout the city.

The late Mickey King, who has a small park named for him at the corner of Hendricks and Greenridge Road, was a guiding influence to the program, as well as a basketball program in the church's gymnasium.

Later, as children of the post-war population grew up in the area, church youth directors took over managing the baseball leagues, which grew to four teams in divisions of tee ball, instructional, tadpole and midget.

In the later part of the 20th century, the area was receiving an influx of young families and the baseball league was growing. The church created the Hendricks Avenue Community Athletic Association to raise money for a new tee ball field and construction of a modern concession stand. Under the leadership of Karl Kronquist, the money was raised and fields named for some of the large donors. Karl was later succeeded by Art Mills and Jon Yost as presidents of the board.

The league grew from about 150 youth playing in the spring to more than 400 playing during the year, with spring and fall seasons. Pastor Kyle Reese has been an enthusiastic supporter of the league, and coached while his sons were playing.

My son began playing in 1989 as a 5-year-old. As the league kept growing, it aligned with national Babe Ruth Association and added a junior age division (ages 13-15) that became one of the most popular with parents. The four team division played most of their games on Friday nights and it became a party atmosphere with families dining at the fields and Matt Carlucci, who had two boys playing, leading the crowd in singing "Take Me Out To The Ball Game" after 4 1/2 innings during the 7-inning games. Coaches who coached several years included Alan Fetner, Mark Huband, Jon Yost, Brooks Andrews and George Foote.

The league was guided by parents, including myself, Elaine and Wayne Mitchell. After several years as Baseball Commissioner, I turned the duties over to Vince Koren, assisted by Tom Dodge. More recently, as Vince's children entered high school, architect Todd Osborn has become commissioner. Vince, with an IT background, guided the league in creating its first website and through online registration. He also was responsible for getting larger batting cages and other field improvements. Todd is continuing to add improvements, with assistance of Doug Oberdorfer and Erik Pietschker, among others.

The entertainment options available to youth have increased to other sports such as flag football and soccer, and to a wide assortment of electronic and computer games. High schools and junior high schools forbid players from playing in recreational leagues, which reduced the players available for junior leagues.

Nonetheless, the league has continued to draw about 100 players each spring for tee ball, 80 for instructional (now called rookie), 60 for tadpole (now called minor) and 40-50 for midgets (now called majors), who sometimes play in a coalition against other leagues in the city. In tee ball alone, the players come from more than 30 schools and preschools.

The league also has advanced teams made up of recreational players who want additional play and they also play against teams from other leagues. It also has all-star teams starting at age 9.

The league's 9-10 year-old all-star team won the district championship and advanced to the state tournament.

As a former baseball commissioner, one of the things that provides great satisfaction is keeping in touch with some parents and players and learning what they are doing. Hendricks baseball players now include at least three doctors, two dentists, several attorneys, data scientists, culinary students, Armed Forces members, oil company managers and numerous other occupations.

Although the league can't claim responsibility for their success, the recreation, often involving parents as well, may help a well-balanced lifestyle which helps lead to success.

Joanelle Wood Mulrain – I remember driving with my Mom in her two-door, dark green Ford convertible from Ortega through Fairfax and past Penny burger, through Avondale and Riverside, half-circling the roundabout in Five Points, and over the original Fuller Warren Bridge into a Southside's San Marco. It was a faraway drive from Ortega's Yacht Club Road where we were the third house built on that dirt road in the early 50s.

Once over the bridge and to the left stood Baptist Hospital (1955), the tall Prudential building and State Bank, then the Acosta Bridge. Tucked-in on the river by the Acosta was The Lobster House Restaurant, where the "Creature of the Black Lagoon" monster movie was made. I remember walking on the wooden plank floors and sitting with my parents in the woven fan-back chairs to wait for a table. They served big Maine lobsters, fresh oysters and Mayport shrimp. Decades later, the restaurant became Someplace Else, where husband

103

Jeff and I had one of our first dates – lobster was still served. We met boxer Joe Frazier there one night at the bar. His hands had fingers as big as Cuba's best cigars.

Mom and I would ride on down San Marco Boulevard, pass the 7-UP plant, now Baptist Outpatient Center, and slip into the famous food joint next door named Texas, known for its lime freezes. Down by the curve was Worman's Deli, the best Jewish bakery in town. Oh, I miss it! Liverwurst. Corned beef. Donut twists. Bagels and lox. Matzo ball soup. Rugelachs. Bear claws. When I had children, we'd order a chocolate birthday cake from Worman's that must have weighed 20 pounds, or so it seemed. They made a Dobash, too. Pearl and her family – we all knew them.

There was great shopping in San Marco Square. "The Mayor of San Marco, I-reeen" Johnson, opened the White's of San Marco door to welcome you. White's had all the latest and greatest books, greeting cards and gifts. "Ree'-nee," we all called her, directed kids to the children's books while the adults went to the hardbacks. Mrs. White was always there, too. The best magazines and newspapers sold in the day were on the multi-tiered wooden shelf. There was no looking inside, you had to "buy to read" – *Life, TIME, Good Housekeeping, Home & Garden*. One high school summer Donna White and I accompanied her mom on a buying trip to Atlanta. We stayed in the new Regency Hyatt Hotel, the famous one with the *first*-in-America glass elevators. We rode them up, down and back up again. It was that very trip "to market" that put retailing in my blood forever.

San Marco had everything, and you shopped with cash. There were no credit cards back then.

Mim's Bakery sold the most delish chocolate eclairs and hot dog buns (bought 'em in eights) in town.

The Silk Shop had bolts of finery – silks, the best wools and cottons, including brocades, and "shark skin" fabrics curled around grey flannel-colored tubes. Every color of the rainbow was featured in the cotton and silk threads wrapped around wooden spools lined up in the proper colorways. You chose the fabric to be "cut"; then it was carefully rolled off the tube and onto the cutting table. A sales lady cut the exact length of your order and gently folded it into a paper bag to take home. There were no plastic bags back then, no "poly" or "ester" fabrics, either. Back home Mom would get out her Singer and cut the new cloth to the exact measurements of the thin, crunchy, noisy paper dress patterns pulled out of a Simplicity or McCall's paper packet.

I saw my first scary movie, "The Shark Hunters", at the San Marco Theatre. It was in color! It was about a man who fell overboard then was cut in half and eaten by a big shark. I had nightmares for years.

The Little Theatre was a special place. I can still smell Mom's Fabergé' Woodhue perfume as she put on her red lipstick, donned a shoulder-padded jacket, slipped her Hanes silk-hosed feet into open-toed lizard shoes, and carried a matching purse, then declared she was "going to the "Theee'-a-tur" with the girls.

The center of the Square had the black wrought iron compass high in the air atop the beautiful white, wedding-cake-like fountain; it's now atop the entrance obelisk. Large cars with real leather and chrome fins would go by with shiny white-walled tires, a status symbol at the time. AM radios were tuned into Virginia Atter Keys on WJAX. Some cars even sported air conditioning. A/C soon came into the shops as well as our house. Wall-to-wall wool carpeting was next. Car seats were leather and one piece from door to door. Bucket seats weren't hot items until the 60s.

In our early teenage years, we pretended to be 16 and quietly pushed a parent's car down a long Ortega driveway in the dark of night to freedom on the highway. We had restricted licenses at 14, which required an adult in the car – ha! Those were the days of sloe gin, six packs of Bud and a couple of Marlboro cigs. We'd put the "foot to the metal" and "catch air" on River Road's famous "Thrill Hill". One night, we nearly hit the big oak tree at the foot of north side of the little water bridge. How did we live through it? We were in hot pursuit of meeting up with our Bolles boyfriends in the dorms. Back then Bolles was a military school and you danced the "Bolles step" in the hallowed halls.

The old Gulf "service" station was owned by Mr. West. Cars used to be serviced – tanks filled with gas, window shields sprayed and wiped clean, including the back one. The gas attendant tucked-in his shirt and wore a belt. He checked the tires, oil, water, and even swept the carpet with a hand broom. Gas was nine, 13, then 27 cents.

There was a bowling alley and a pharmacy. Pic N Save was on the corner. Across the street Geisenhof's offered fine linens, crystal and gifts. Stand n' Snack had great sandwiches and hot French fries. We all went to Underwood's to dream at the diamonds. And, who can forget Peterson's Five & Dime where we picked out Easter chicks and silk flowers upstairs. If Utsey's in Avondale didn't have your shoe size, you popped over to their shop in San Marco for those red, white or navy

106

blue leather 2' heels with pointed toes for church. San Marco is still full of churches. In 1978 Jeff and I were married in the little deconsecrated 1888 Episcopal Church moved from down river to MOSH, then moved to San Marco's public park.

Some may remember walking into American National Bank as a patron and being served orange juice in a paper cup from a rolling cart by a man in a coat and tie. Imagine that! And, the columned Fire Station is a historical landmark and sits proudly in the same place as it continues to serve us all.

If you had dry cleaning or something special needed tending to, like bridal gown cleaning, off it went to Herman Jackson's. Their two-story, electric belt moved up and down. Clothes under clear plastic were filed alpha on hangers and hooked into the belt. Cardboard was put inside starched shirts and wrapped in plastic, too. Jackson's is taking care of yet another generation today on the other side of the Square.

New stores and restaurants soon replaced the old. The first Peterbrooke opened. I bought my antique Venice painting in Bounds Cave from Judy Blumberg. Ward and Forrest opened The Ward Room, still a trend-setting, beautiful shop. The Town Pump changed into a trendy new restaurant and bar.

Down the street was Ye Old Time Tavern, a rusty hangout kinda place with an indoor shuffleboard game, served up great greasy burgers, cold beers and music. We called it the YOTT Club.

Married and living on Alhambra Drive, we raised both boys in San Marco. Jeffry (1985) and John (1991) still call it "home". They always had a secret envelope in Pizza Palace so when they showed up without any money on them after school or ball practice, they were covered.

Now, the Square has fancy brick walkways, public sculpture, a three-lion fountain, and it continues to be a magnet for families, cultural activities and shopping. We have a Mulrain brick somewhere on the Square. It's a special place. New babies are pushed around again by young parents. Time flies. My kids are grown and gone now, but we call San Marco home.

San Marco – a place in time for a generation of memories for the Mulrain family. We love San Marco.

Sandy Myers – My parents lived in Lakewood when I was born. We moved to Arlington so my Dad could be closer to his business, Edwards Pipe & Tobacco Shop. I worked in the shop after school and through college. I always liked San Marco so I opened a second location there for my Dad in 1983. I called it Edwards of San Marco. My store had three different locations on San Marco Blvd as my business prospered and grew. All my customers became friends with my main assistant Judy, a sweet Jack Russell. Edwards and Judy both have bricks at the lion fountain. I had a little apartment on San Marco Blvd until I fulfilled my dream when I bought a home a few blocks from the square. I hosted many "shop" parties at my bungalow for my customers and friends who had become part of my family. After 24 years, I sold the store so I would have time to take care of my parents. Several years later I opened a new store, My Best Friend's Closet, also on San Marco Blvd. This women's clothing store was in two different locations in the square. Most of my life has been centered in San Marco and now that I'm retired and traveling, I always look for quaint communities like San Marco wherever I go. Some have come close, but San Marco is still the best place to call home.

Ben Oberdorfer, 5th grade – My experience playing baseball at Hendricks Avenue Baseball League (HAB) was a good one. I played there for six years. I started in tee-ball and finished in kid pitch. One of my favorite parts was playing for the HAB All-Star team. I played All-Stars for three seasons. My first two seasons were tough. We did not win a lot of games. In 2016, Coach Jay Kaplan took over as the head coach. He decided we needed a fresh start. He changed our team colors back to green and gold and changed our name to the "Hendricks Angels." Players were selected after a tryout. Our practices were long and had lots of running. I did not enjoy all of the running. I especially did not like when we had to run around the entire field with our bats over our heads. We played scrimmage doubleheaders against other parks to help us prepare for the District Tournament. We won most of these games. Winning those first games boosted our morale.

Our first tournament was at Ft. Caroline. We won our two "seeding games" and earned the number one seed. We won our first game in the elimination. We lost to Normandy in the semi-finals. I was bummed that we did not win the tournament, but was excited to have gone as far as we did.

We played in the Julington Creek All Star Classic next. Again, we won our seeding games and earned the top seed. This time, we won the tournament. I was so excited to win for HAB and my teammates. The trophy presentation was funny because the trophy we won looked like the one from the World Cup in soccer. We joked we had won the "Baseball World Cup."

After that tournament, it was time to get ready for the District Tournament. It was hosted by San Jose Athletic Association. They are our rivals because their park is close to ours. The tournament was double elimination. It was very important to win our first game to get momentum and not have to play as many games. Our first game was against the Villages Baseball Club. We had played them in a scrimmage earlier in the season and split our games with them. In the District Tournament, we got down by three runs in the first inning. In the next to last inning, we were down three runs. I came up with runners on second and third bases. I hit a slow roller (a "dinker") in front of the pitcher. My first thought was, "Oh no, I'm out!" But the pitcher overthrew the first baseman and the two runs scored. I came around to score and tie the game on a wild pitch. We won the game 7 to 6. Our next game was against San Jose. They had eliminated our team in the District Tournament two years earlier. We beat them 4-3. I had three hits and three RBIs. That win put us in the championship game. We had to play San Jose again. That game was not as close. We beat them 9-4. Nine of our players had hits in that game. The day before the championship, Coach Jay had us practice on how we would celebrate if we won. When we got the last out we all ran to the pitcher's mound and celebrated. It felt awesome to win for HAB. It was the first time an HAB 10U team had won the District Championship. We were able to represent our little park in the State Tournament. I will always be proud of my HAB team.

John Peyton – I am very fortunate to have spent time in every corner of Jacksonville. While each area within our vast city has its own distinct and attractive characteristics, it is San Marco that drew us in and where we chose to live and raise our family.

San Marco is a gem, a community that is essentially in the middle of everything, but still maintains its tranquility. Much of the credit for this goes to the city planners of decades ago. While creating the city of South Jacksonville, the name for the area of San Marco before it was annexed into Jacksonville in the early 30s, a focus was placed on creating a community with walkable, tree-lined streets, abundant parks and greenspace, generous river views and a supportive commercial district. Compared to many neighborhoods that developed around Jacksonville in the decades that followed, this became a rarity.

We are also an eclectic compilation of architecture. While other neighborhoods have historical buildings, you'd be hard pressed to find another area in Jacksonville that contains the diversity that we have in San Marco. From cottages and bungalows to castles and mansions, there is a home for everyone in San Marco and each one adds to our character and charm.

But, while the infrastructure makes us unique, the people make us special. All ages, incomes and backgrounds come together in San Marco. Whether its community red wagon parades and pot lucks, or church holiday events, or friends meeting to experience the incredible dining and shopping, people come from all over to experience San Marco. And we, as residents, are proud of our neighborhood and are happy to share.

These are just some of the things that attracted my wife, Kathryn, and me to San Marco and the things we see continuing to get even better with time.

Jim Price – The FBI transferred our family to Jacksonville Florida from Buffalo New York in the fall of 1972. What a change from freezing cold and snow to the sunshine of Florida. We took a temporary apartment on River Road. Very quickly we determined that San Marco was really home.

We had to tell our real estate agent to stop sending us to the new housing developments on the south- side as we were more interested in the 1930s style homes in San Marco. In April 1973 we purchased a three bedroom two bath brick 1930s style home on Northwood Road, with a backyard that joined the Hendricks Avenue elementary school playground. Our neighbors were very friendly. We could not have found a better location as the duck pond was just across the street.

The San Marco shopping area reminded us of our local hometowns in small-town Ohio and North Alabama. It suited us just fine. Most memorable was the San Marco Theater where we were reminded of 1930s style movie houses from our hometowns. We remember specifically seeing a movie titled "The Apprenticeship of Duddy Kravitz" at the San Marco Theater. It was an early movie of future superstar, Richard Dreyfuss.

Herman Jacksons' Atomic Cleaners was where we had our dry cleaning done. Mr. Jackson had invented a new cleaning process that he called atomic cleaning. You could always rely on a great cleaning job and especially spot removals that were a specialty of Herman Jackson's.

On the corner where the current Firehouse Subs is located was a tire store that would meet all of your needs for your car. Across the street was the Pic 'N Save. This became a favorite shopping spot as they carried just about everything one might want to buy.

Peterson's variety store was next to the San Marco Theater. It too was a favorite shopping spot for those sundries and miscellaneous items for various holidays during the year and to repair anything that needed repairing.

Across Hendricks Avenue was the American Bank that was locally owned. It too was a favorite place to meet all our business needs.

In April 1974, we became members of Southside Baptist Church. We remained members of this congregation until we left Jacksonville in 1980. San Marco was still a thriving local center when we returned in 1994. Soon after, however, the Pic 'N Save went out of business, Herman Jackson's also, the San Marco Theater was in the doldrums and the American Bank was sold.

Beginning at about 2000, we could see San Marco turning the corner and once again becoming the focal point of the community. With a lot of work and effort by a lot of people, San Marco slowly began coming back again as a favorite place to go. It took several years, but it is now a place to go.

We rejoined Southside Baptist Church in 1994 and have been there ever since seeking to be a part of the community serving San Marco and the Southside area.

Scott Riley – Owner of Stellers Gallery

Twenty-Four Years! It's hard to believe we opened Stellers Gallery twenty-four years ago this September in 1992. The San Marco community welcomed us with open arms and the memories are too many to share them all.

I've always said that San Marco Square was the crown jewel of Jacksonville. The family owned businesses and wonderful restaurants, the coffee shop and wine bar gave so much to those that enjoyed the square.

Although Starbucks took away any small coffee shop, its presence (especially to my daily habit) is a great place to meet friends or conduct business.
I have, like so many, loved and appreciated the landscape facelift we got the last year. Its openness gives the impression of warmth and friendliness.

My fondest memories are of my children growing up in the gallery running around and eating the candy that has been a signature of Stellers Gallery. Now, my seven grandchildren are running around as it's become a perfect place for their parents to drop off for Grandpa to watch!

Thank you San Marco friends for your twenty-four years of support and patronage. Happy 90th!

Parker Roberson, 6th grade – I'm Parker and I attended Hendricks Avenue Elementary, and this summer we took a field trip for Ambassadors (Ambassadors are chosen representatives of our school that help open car doors, clean classrooms, and patrol the hallways. Ambassadors are the student leaders of HAE). This field trip has been a tradition for

114

many years. Some of the highlights of the trip are visits to the National Air and Space Museum, Busch Gardens, Old Williamsburg and the 9/11 Memorial. I personally had a great time because my family came, many friends were there, and the trip was well planned. I am delighted I was able to attend this valuable trip that has been going on for many years.

The Washington D.C. trip did require funding, though. The parents, staff, and ambassadors of Hendricks worked extremely hard on the Christmas tree lot to raise money for the trip. They also sold flowers and poinsettias to raise money for the trip. This conveys that going on the D.C. trip does take a lot of work, money and time and it's worth it. I want to acknowledge everyone who made this trip possible and thank them for making it happen.

I liked the Air and Space Museum because of Albert Einstein's planetarium and the flight simulator. This flight simulator was not an ordinary flight simulator, though. This one is able to go upside down! Cool! I rode it with my friend named Trey Seeker.

Old Williamsburg was very different from regular civilization because there were many rules for the residents, such as not allowing people to see your TV through your window, and staying in character. But it was very interesting seeing everyone in character.

The 9/11 memorial was highly artistic to behold, because it had benches organized in a way so that you can tell if the person died on the plane or in the pentagon. I believed the designer of that memorial did an extraordinary job.

I am pleased that the trip planners who created the itinerary added in the stop at Busch Gardens. It was a magnificent closing for the trip. The rides were thrilling and mammoth. I'm glad I was able to tell about my amazing trip to Washington. I enjoyed it a lot and made memories that will last a lifetime.

Jay Robinson – San Marco Memories –

My family and I were parishioners of Assumption Catholic Church when it was located on Gary Street. The church was demolished in 1954 to make way for the interstate and the Fuller Warren Bridge. The church then moved to its present location on Atlantic Boulevard and Assumption School occupied the former offices of Merrill Stevens Shipbuilding. The shipyards were torn down and the football field and school for Bishop Kenny were built in its place.

I attended Landon High when I was in 9th grade while awaiting the construction of Catholic Central High (Bishop Kenny) so I got to know a number of students from Landon. I remember that their football practice field was FEC Park (Alexandria Oaks Park). Once I moved on to Bishop Kenny in 10th grade, Landon was our huge rival in football and they were pretty darn tough. Landon won the state football championship in 1954. The following year we had a huge celebration when we beat Landon, the defending state champs!

A party took place in my friend, Conrad Gunti's, garage on Marco Place one night. The famous rock and roll singer Johnny Tillotson (Google him if you need to refresh your memory) showed up and put on a show for everyone. The teenage girls were quite impressed, but the boys not so much as

116

they were jealous of Johnny flirting with their girls!

My friends and I used to sneak into Oriental Gardens to play. Mostly we played hide and seek to avoid detection by the groundskeeper who lived there.

Besides hanging out in the woods and hanging out on the river, our Saturday entertainment (after doing chores) was going to San Marco Square to the movies and go bowling. Admission to the theater was 25 cents.

Growing up in the 50's was wonderful - full of freedom and adventure. Ah, the good ole days!

Robin Robinson – I moved to Jacksonville in 1984. The first time I saw the Square I found it instantly intriguing. It wasn't nearly as beautiful as it is today, but its charm was undeniable. There was a funny triangular shaped dirt lot in the middle of the square where people parked at random with a defunct fountain nearby painted with bright sunflowers in an effort to somehow resurrect a thing of beauty. The sidewalks were made up of hexagonal shapes which were dangerous to traverse in certain spots. The San Marco building and the shops with their funky fronts like "Out to Lunch" and "Edwards Pipe Shop" completed the picture.

It was in this setting that the San Marco Master Plan was created. The first order of business was to plant trees to create a canopy, then to address issues such as uneven sidewalks and a broken fountain. Since that time many improvements have taken place to make the Square what it is today. It is a place I have come to love and enjoy on a daily basis. It makes me proud to call San Marco home.

117

Once I became aware of the history of San Marco and South Jacksonville I was led to dig deeper into its story. With the renovation of the South Jacksonville City Hall and the celebratory grand opening which took place in early 2008, I found many descendants of the city fathers still living nearby. They opened up their family picture albums and their family stories which led to the publication of *Southbank Sojourn: A Photographic Journey through the Early Days of South Jacksonville and San Marco.* The Southbank of the St. Johns River occupied a unique place in history as the gateway to the development of the east coast of Florida which I find fascinating.

Debra Webb Rogers – Everything You Can Walk To

San Marco is a small town nestled in a big city, a walkable area of beautiful contrasts. It is a mosaic of whispered histories hidden in familiar places. Like the gazebo in Balis Park whose circular design echoes the shape of the tiny Gulf gas station that stood in almost the same spot in the 1920s. Or the still-visible rise of land in Alexandria Oaks (FEC) Park that was once the pitcher's mound on the baseball field used by Landon High School students. In San Marco the past rubs shoulders with the present without compromising either. This is part of what makes San Marco so enticing. Then there are the people...

When I moved here in the 1970s, my neighbors were those of the "Greatest Generation", some of whom were born in the very houses they still lived in. They generously shared their stories, bestowing upon me a poignant legacy of San Marco memories. They described savoring succulent treats from *Mim's Bakery*, meeting girls at *Skateland,* and spending afternoons watching cars with license plates from far-flung states speed south down Kings Avenue. They laughed about a mean bull in a neighbor's back pasture that challenged their youthful bravado. Their stories have woven themselves into my own memories - memories that include things like shopping at Pic N Save (for everything from motor oil to mascara), grabbing a bite (standing up) at Stand N Snack, or pausing (perplexed) beside a dry fountain covered in a Plexiglas dome.

San Marco is a deeply beloved area. Whether you were born here, arrived yesterday, or returned after a long absence, it is *home.* This intangible sensation of home permeates everything in San Marco. It is what drew me in the first day I arrived and explored the small rose garden in Fletcher Park. This feeling, this sense of home, is difficult to pin down and even more difficult to put into words. Home has been described in various ways by writers and poets, but one quote that depicts San Marco beautifully is this one, by children's author Jerry Spinelli: *"Home is everything you can walk to."*

You can walk anywhere and everywhere in San Marco, just as the first residents did in the 1920s. You can see a play, watch a movie, buy a book, drink a latté, listen to a band, relax by a fountain, have an elegant dinner or meet friends for pizza. You can sit by the river, walk to pocket parks, attend an art show… or a wedding.

My husband and I were married in Fletcher Park, the first Sunday after the historic Carpenter Gothic Church was relocated there. The reception was held in our San Marco home, and the guests and bridal party strolled there from the church.

History. Memories. *Home.* Everything you can walk to…

John A. Rush, III – My grandfather, John A. Rush, was already a prominent Jacksonville attorney when he and Ada Louise (Simpson) moved the family in 1941 from 50 acres in Mandarin where Julington Creek met with the St Johns River to the white neoclassical house at 2503 River Road. When they first moved to Jacksonville, they had lived "on the other side of the river" where Ada Louise had family, including her brother Bryan Simpson, who would later play a major role in Jacksonville history as the presiding judge of the U.S. Middle District of Florida case during the desegregation of Duval County Schools. Mandarin had provided plenty of room for the young family and Granddad's hobby of breeding English Pointers for field trials. But when the "big house" in Mandarin burned to the ground, it was time to move back into town. Thinking they would go back to Ortega, it was the grand house and extra lot, combined with proximity to downtown via Main Street, that prompted them to consider the newly reinvigorated area of San Marco. The US was still not officially in the War, but Roosevelt's promise of material support meant the nearby shipyards in St. Nicholas were starting to hum and Jacksonville was recovering from the Depression.

The house at 2503 River Road was in the 1st Addition Better Homes Section of San Marco (aka Villa Alexandria) which featured bigger lots and curved streets; a new concept when platted. The house was built in 1937 for attorney Fred and Norma Kent, it was the fifth house to be built along the east side of the street between River Oaks and Arbor Lane. The house was spacious with four bedrooms upstairs and two family bathrooms. Like all the homes in the development as required by covenant, the house had live-in space for the maid. The extra lot facing Maple Street provided plenty of room for Granddad's dogs. San Marco was convenient to his work, and good schools (Bolles Military Academy and Bartram School

120

for Girls (now Bolles Middle School Campus)). When my father, John Jr., met my mother, Betty Ann Green, in college in Atlanta, it was to 2503 River Road that he brought his bride-to-be to meet her future in-laws before their 1951 wedding. In 1953, before the birth of her first grandchild in September, Ada Louise passed away.

Granddad met Clara Upchurch while lobbying in Tallahassee; they connected, among other reasons, over their enthusiasm for the Florida Gators. His new bride moved to 2503 River Road in 1954. In 1959, the house again was filled with young laughter as my aunt, Lois Clare, expanded the family. That same year, the extra lot was sold to Dr. Aaron Oberdorfer to build a house at 930 Maple Lane. In 1970, a downstairs bedroom suite, now a cozy family room with a very unique bar, was added. Granddad died in 1981, having lived forty-years in the same San Marco house. In 1994, Clara transferred the house to Lois. Lois added a master suite to the back upstairs and has made other updates, but the beautiful traditional facade remains just as architect Roy A. Benjamin designed it, now complimented by a corner lawn of blooming flowers and trees planted and maintained by San Marco's famed Julia Canipelli of Julia's Digs.

My parents started their family on the first day of class at Emory Medical School and added two more children while Dad was finishing his medical education. When it was time to establish a medical practice in 1960, returning to Jacksonville was a logical career choice. With the growing Baptist Hospital complex in San Marco, the south side of Jacksonville was to be home. My parents bought a home just south of Lakewood on Sweet Briar Lane. But in 1963, expecting her fifth (and final) child, my mother became enthralled with the "For Sale" sign at 2311 Laurel Road. Built in 1939 and known as the Wolfson

Estate, the one-acre corner property included a tennis court and room for a pool which our family soon added. 2311 Laurel was a grand family home designed by Hopkins & Huddleston. With a bedroom for each child, living quarters for the appreciated live-in help, a conversation-starting elevator, and plenty of space for gatherings, Mom diligently lobbied my Dad and got help from her father to make the $40,000.00 purchase. Shortly after moving in, we found a small (2'x2'x2') safe in a back bedroom; the contents included Bills of Sale of scrap steel to the Japanese by the Morris Wolfson owned Florida Pipe & Supply, but no one knows why the safe had been left behind.

A few years later, first cousins moved in to 1025 Maple Lane (built in 1938 for David and Lulu Halpern) where the extended family gathered for many years at Thanksgiving. Elizabeth McCoy and husband Johnny raised four boys and a girl in the house before selling in 1985. Rush's ran from River Road to Laurel Road in abundance. Forays to Peterson's or Pic-n-Save, on foot or by bicycle were common occurrences. San Jose Boulevard was four-lanes from San Marco to Baymeadows. The Fuller Warren Bridge required a toll to go to Riverside/Ortega. More than one Wednesday evening you could see Betty Ann and her five children walk to the big white church (Southside Baptist) on the Square. (Dad squired the family by car on Sundays.) 2311 Laurel Road was the site for numerous church parties as well as school-related socials, garden club meetings and medical society soirees. 2311 Laurel Road hosted the wedding reception for my sister (and Fred Legere) in July 1977, and rehearsal dinners for Pam (Turbow) and me in April 1980 and brother Carl and Ann (Gibson) in June 1981. With all of their children out of the house, my parents sold 2311 Laurel Road in 1982.

After seventeen years in Tampa, my own family elected to come back for our son to be the third John Rush to graduate from Bolles (1949, 1973, and 2009). We naturally had San Marco as our first choice of neighborhoods. In 2003 we purchased the house at 2344 Laurel Road. We did not target living across from my childhood home, but it was nice to look out the kitchen window to recall great memories and over our back fence to remember all the time at my Aunt and Uncle's. Built in 1945, the one-story brick was designed by D. Floyd Rosser for George and Elizabeth Wood. Mr. Wood owned Independent Furniture Company and provided materials to the shipyards. When we had the house inspected, we were told the building materials, including roof timbers, were worthy of a fortress. One of the most unique features on the house are the fancy exposed eave tails; the house originally had a flat-tile clay roof which unfortunately was replaced with asphalt shingles in the 1980s. The Woods family enclosed the back porch. There had been three interim owners who had made modest changes and updates, including adding a pool but, thankfully, leaving the original 1945 tile in three bathrooms. While working diligently with architect Robert Porter to retain the original exterior appearance on the 2/3 acre property, we increased the number of bathrooms as well as updating the kitchen and other areas. We too walked to Southside Baptist and the Square, but now visiting The Loop and Starbuck's. 2344 was the site of several church socials and Bolles Soccer team dinners. In 2013, with our son making his home in Charlotte, we decided it was time to down-size. But we were not ready to leave San Marco.

Pam and I now live at 2782 Green Bay Lane. Green Bay was part of the original San Jose Parks plat filed in 1928; in 1935 Whatley, Davin & Company replatted the section just south of Villa Alexandria with smaller lots and began to have success with lot sales. Our house was built in 1937 for Joseph and Isabel Mallett. Now a two-story white stucco, we think it

123

started as brick, possibly just one-story. We have little evidence except for the foundation walls visible under the added front terrace. The River Oaks covenants did not require space for live-in help as did the larger lots in Villa Alexandria, but construction cost had to be at least $4000.00 west of Hendricks and $2500 east of Hendricks with a minimum 25' set back. Many of the homes in River Oaks were designed by Ivan Smith, a founding partner of Reynolds, Smith & Hills. After at least four major modifications over many years, 2782 Green Bay now has four bedrooms, four baths, formal areas and more. An unusual feature is the small cellar; not uncommon in Riverside/Avondale, but rare on the south side of the river. We had walked throughout San Marco for years, but not until we purchased this house did we learn that the 1935 subdivision plat included a road at the south end to connect Green Bay, Riverwood, White Oak and West Cove rather than the realized dead-end configuration. Whether it was topography or budget constraints, Brookway Road was never built and its easement is now part of River Oaks Park.

We still love to walk to the Square, walk to Southside Baptist, or just walk past beautiful homes under magnificent oaks. We enjoy waiving to long-time neighbors, seeing new families, and admiring improvements and enhancements. The proximity to excellent health care, sports venues, museums, theaters, the airport, and the interstate to go North, South or West, cannot be beat. I am so grateful Granddad had the wisdom 75 years ago to choose San Marco for his home.

Karen Saltmarsh – South Jacksonville Presbyterian Preschool has been a part of the San Marco neighborhood since 1953 and is a ministry of South Jacksonville Presbyterian Church. It is a small, family-oriented preschool that allows moms the opportunity to have a safe place for their children ages one to five to interact with peers and receive a top-notch education. I first came here as a parent. My children Ernie, Emily, and Grace all attended SJPP. Soon after I fell in love with this school, I began teaching in the 4's – a story similar to many teachers at our school. Recently my career came full circle, as I returned as the director in 2015. It was like coming home. Every teacher we currently have on staff has had their children enrolled here, and we currently even have eight grandchildren attending – including my granddaughter Eloise. Friendships are made, and it becomes an easy decision for parents to want to stay with us. Many things about our school have evolved through the years. With the changes in education, we have adapted to provide a stimulating program that promotes a child's intellectual curiosity. We introduced Handwriting Without Tears, sight words, resources such as Spanish and Multicultural Day, and more. We extended our after school program hours to meet needs of working parents. We have added classes to reduce class size and better accommodate age differences. Despite these changes, we have thrived in keeping our traditions intact. From the annual Easter parade through the Square to our Thanksgiving Feast, family and community are at the center of our school. Currently teachers have a combined 98 years of teaching experience, and it is evident in all they do that they love their students and take pride in their work and school. SJPP is in the business of growing children into lifelong learners!

Suzanne Saltmarsh – There is a saying "Life turns on a dime"

For me this saying has never been about the amount or sum. It has always been about the actual significance of the exact spot; the space and time. Applied to life, it spoke directly to me about relationships and connections that serendipitously occur in a specific and significant moment. And within that specificity, a genuine connection is made that has the ability to affect change and influence a life forever.

That is what dance is for me.

Choreography is the vehicle that allows life to be revealed for me as an artist. San Marco was my first place of significance. I grew up behind the San Marco movie theater on Largo Road with my six brothers and sisters. My dancing began at an early age learning from my two older sisters. I would recruit as many siblings or friends in the neighborhood to put on small dance concerts ; whether it be in the front yard or in the park next to what I called the tadpole fountain. Many of the small parks throughout San Marco as well as the San Marco Lake became great sources of inspiration and imagination for choreography. The beautiful majestic oaks created the natural proscenium for lovely spontaneous dance festivals in the early 1970's. San Marco set the stage for a fascination with site-specific work as well as choreography that bridges together nature and social issues.

Many of the strong features, of San Marco, can be seen today in my choreography. I often have images of oaks or water, like the St. Johns River or the Atlantic Ocean. As a backdrop for my ballets. I find that one's childhood is represented in our initial quilt and as we journey on in life we add onto that quilt. It grows in richness, texture, and color. The dance becomes the story of our quilt. I want Dance to touch people. I have always wanted a response from the viewer. That desire springs from my relationship to the small San Marco community that I grew up in ...with the backdrop of nature, beauty, architecture, natural waterways, and the gentle kindness of my neighbors. My upbringing and surroundings in San Marco was the specific, genuine connection that made the difference in my life with dance.

Lindsay Shilling – Growing up in San Marco suited me so well that as a grown-up, I did not go far. My husband and I are raising our family one street over from my childhood home.

San Marco is more than a neighborhood for me. It is part of who I am. My first job, was babysitting for families in the neighborhood. And as a grown-up, my only jobs were at advertising agencies in the neighborhood. The first board I had the pleasure serving on was San Marco Preservation Society. Our neighbors are more than just neighbors, they are like family.

As a child, there were always hidden spots for us to play in. We thought they were super-secret and no one knew about them, which made it even more appealing. There were makeshift bridges over creeks, swings hanging from trees that didn't appear to be in anyone's yard, a dock that didn't really seem to belong to anyone and the secret path to the duck pond neighborhood. These were our stomping grounds and it felt like they belonged only to us. No one asked how the swings got there or who built those little wooden bridges. We just knew those areas were ours to play in.

As a grown-up, I still don't know whose swings we were swinging on or if we were supposed to be out on that dock. And I don't want to know, so please don't tell me. Some of those childhood bridges have rotted away, the dock has fallen down, and the swings have disappeared. But the neighborhood provides and my children continue to find their own secret spots. New swings have popped up, new shops and restaurants are in The Square. And the novelty of a restaurant actually in a movie theatre is just as thrilling to my children as it was to me.

Throughout all my years living here, one thing has remained constant. The people. And they are what mean the most to me. Our neighbors take great pride in their homes and the neighborhood, not just the way it looks but the way it feels. There is always something happening on our streets. We happily share our neighborhood with people from all over the city. This makes the sense of community among those who live here all the more meaningful. And it's that sense of community that makes San Marco.

Jon Singleton – San Marco has a kind of stickiness. You don't notice it at first, but it gradually sucks you in. Before you know it, you become intertwined with the whole history and legacy of people that have come before you. You start to get involved, first with stores and restaurants, then schools and churches. If you're lucky, you go deep and connect with community organizations and get a glimpse of the glue that holds everything together. One day, someone will ask you to lead a small group at church, or become a Cub Scout Den leader. The next thing you know, 10 years have passed and you get to attend the graduation ceremonies for your young protégées, and you realize that you'll be at their weddings as well.

I started in Cub Scout Pack 35 with my son in 2007. We had almost 40 First Grade boys, in several Dens, and they had extremely short attention spans. At the time, they were only able to focus on rowdy games and sugar. That fall we got to go camping and introduce the boys to the wilderness where the main attractions were fire, knives and dirt. My son was hooked! It was hard to see the philosophical goal of Scouting was to build character through successive personal accomplishments, but we can see it now. The Pack, chartered through Southside Methodist is part of the larger Troop 35 (the older boys), and has been in existence since 1921. Its resources are incredible, including both the numerous volunteers and equipment collected over the years. Those blessings, along with decades of organizational knowledge have honed this amazing organization that introduces adventure and life skills into the lives of young men, resulting in the calibration of a moral compass to help them navigate the world.

In 2010, I was asked to lead the Pack of 120 rambunctious boys, and with the help of their parents orchestrate the many activities we tried to accomplish. As crazy as my 2-year stint was, that's remained my absolute favorite volunteer job of all time, and it was definitely the most rewarding.

The best example I can think of in the ways Scouting creates fun, while sneaking in great lessons is the Pinewood Derby. I still have the car I made with my Grandfather in the 70's, and we raced it against the cars my son and I made. The Derby itself is a great spectacle, and there's fierce competition (sometimes between the Dads!). Unlike most of society today, there are clear winners and trophies. And there are also tears. But, at some point, everyone realizes the true reward is the shared experience and accomplishment of making and racing the car. Everyone actually does win.

I've now been involved in Scouting for 10 years as an adult, and my little boy is taller than me. We've now traversed the Canadian wilderness by canoe, and backpacked for weeks in the Rockies, and shared experiences with his comrades. I've guided the young men through storms and medical emergencies and have found a wonderful way to pass on decision making and leadership is learned in the Navy. I can't imagine finding a better place to do that, than through our own Scout Pack and Troop at Southside Methodist in San Marco.

Doug Skiles – I've been asked by many, most from other neighborhoods, how did San Marco manage to build a park at a time when the city could barely afford to mow the grass? In large part I believe we can thank the Great Recession of 2008 for the expansion of Balis Park that was completed in 2013.

The San Marco Boulevard Streetscape project was conceived, designed and funded under the administration of Mayor John Peyton in 2008 as one of the last projects before the City of Jacksonville's budget woes put the brakes on most public projects. The initial budget was based on construction costs before the recession hit, but the project was awarded post-recession when most road builders were hungry and looking for work.

This timing provided the streetscape project with a healthy contingency budget, one that was used to accelerate the re-opening of the road along the north segments and later provided the funding needed to extend the project into San Marco Square. The original design stopped with the roundabout at Naldo Street, just north of the Square.
A second factor influenced by the recession was that many of the volunteers (myself included) had a bit more free time on their hands.

In 2011, I moved our engineering business into an upstairs office owned by Keith Kimball. The office space is great, but the only place to park is in Southside Baptist Church's parking lot north of the Square. This meant having to cross an intersection with three pedestrian walk signals (and only one worked reliably). Much of my motivation was spurred by our newly elected Council Member, Lori Boyer, when after hearing me complain about the broken walk signals, challenged me to come up with a better design (in other words, stop complaining and become part of the solution). And oh by the way, we may be able to get a little extra money from the streetscape project that is currently still under budget.

I doodled a few concepts but couldn't come up with anything that would make a significant impact. A few days later, I sat in an Urban Land Institute meeting with the engineer for the streetscape project, Wayne Reed, and he pitched an idea to me (which he actually did draw on a napkin). The light bulb went off and I went to his office immediately following the event to discuss it in more detail with his design staff.

They explained to me, that instead of having two major roads merge into one, we should send everyone around the Square in a clockwise direction that would function like a larger, irregularly shaped roundabout. And, if we wanted, we could use the space in between to expand the park.

The first two people I talked to in the neighborhood were Rob Smith and Keith Kimball. They liked it. The three of us went to see Zim Boulos. He liked it. Then the four of us went to see Lori. We needed a consensus, and I have learned from experience that is best built in one-on-one meetings. Once we had Lori's blessing (who's next words were – you better find a way to pay for it), we started meeting with George

Foote of the San Marco Merchants Association and Diane Martin and Mary Toomey of San Marco Preservation Society. Both groups jumped in and assisted greatly with donations of time and money.

The last hurdle of approval was the City's Public Works Department. Fortunately, we were armed with a mass of local public support, private donations and the knowledge that the streetscape project had a few bucks left over. The director, Jim Robinson, was a traffic engineer who loved traffic modeling (they all do), so we hired a local traffic engineer to create a model. Jim saw the value in our proposal and worked with Lori to get the final approvals from the city.

In about six months, the project went from concept, to approved, to funded.

Dr. Mary Soha – "Blessed Footnotes"
I had gone to many neighborhood meetings when looking to move to a large house in 1992. We had just gone from 4 to 6 boys, their combined energies were somewhere around Mach 7, and I knew I would need a bigger kitchen. We kept looking back to San Marco. The people, the location, the history and the traditions gave it such a "small town" feeling. The house we fell in love with was everything we needed and so much more. The previous owner and I had many things in common- our children went to the same school, we loved old homes and we both had teen boys. The sale was made, and just before closing in December, she added that there was one more thing she needed to mention and that this was an "assumed" part of the deed. The neighborhood Live Nativity took place on her front yard the second weekend in December and she hoped that this could continue.

132

Our first year (and the neighborhood's fifth year) of the Live Nativity was amazing! The neighbors all took turns, costuming across the street, taking their positions, and being witness to the mystery of Christmas. We had heard stories of previous years of camels that spit at the shepherds and elephants that had gone wild, but out first year there was such a calmness you could sense the beauty of the night.

We learned the Nativity was started by a group of neighbors that wanted to "give something back" in thanksgiving for all the blessings they had received. One gentleman had been a P.O.W., tortured, but was returned home. He went through rehab, and with the support of his wife, became a successful commercial realtor. I believe it was this family that was one of the driving forces for this event.

Over the years neighborhood children have played roles from angels to Mary and Joseph. Men have volunteered as shepherds and Wise Men. Women have dressed the characters, served hot chocolate and everyone has helped with set up and cleanup. There have been years when the angels have flown away, cows have gotten loose and gone through the neighborhood, and baby sheep have "stolen the show "but always, the sacredness and the wonder of that night 2000 years ago is felt as neighbors and friends share this event.

It has been our privilege to participate in this event for 23 years. Hopefully this is a tradition that will carry on for many more. And the location... well, that's the "footnote" in our deed and what a "Blessed Footnote" it is.

Merry Christmas!

Niki Stokes – Owner of Studio K Dance

I wish I could fill this page with all the images and memories of the amazing San Marco youth I have taught over the years. It is as if a photograph is taken of them the instant we are introduced. Even as I help a student prepare for the Miss Senior High Pageant, I can still picture her exactly how she was over a decade ago! I have had the pleasure to meet these wonderful children in so many unique and wonderful settings. Camp Theatre Jax, LaVilla School of the Arts, an area preschool or teaching them at the studio…their chubby-cheeked faces fills my mind's eye!

I love how every moment is new, honest, and exciting. It is such a privilege to be a part of their journey at every age. Watching them learn how to master a technical aspect of dance or figuring out how to maneuver their little pinky finger while singing, "Where is Thumbkin"…the struggle is real my friends! The satisfaction they get from problem solving (on their own) and learning to conquer something bigger is invaluable. The sense of accomplishment is palpable and the look on their face is priceless! It is about more than just dance. It is about developing qualities every child needs to succeed!

Thank you to the supportive community members of San Marco. I have enjoyed seeing YOU too over the years! Every recital, showcase, and public performance…you all have been there to support these youngsters! Your applause fuels this generation forward. Whether they become professionals in the performing arts or move to become a Mother, Author, CEO, Lawyer or Doctor…you being there has made a difference.

To be even the *smallest* part of a child's life is a *tremendous* honor and I have truly been given a precious gift.

Thank you San Marco!

Rod Sullivan – My wife Ellen and I moved to San Marco twenty-five years ago. One of the things we like most is the amount of "public art" there is in the Square, and how much more has been added since we moved here. Permit me to elaborate.

It may be unfair to pick a favorite, but we have one. It is Gary Lee Price's bronze sculpture entitled "Windy Days." The three children, chasing their kites, and followed by their trusty and playful puppy, is a favorite of children, who are attracted to it like moths to a light. On any given Friday night you'll see kids climbing on the base, posing with the bronze children, and pretending that they too are flying kites. It's a magical piece. Price, a 60 year old Utah-based sculptor, has a whole series of children's art, but even among the series, "Windy Days" stands out as a favorite, and it's right here in Balis Park.

The most well-known piece of art is the landmark in the Square--the three lions. Tell anyone that "you'll meet them by the lions" and they are sure to find you. Hugh Bradford Nicholson has created other Florida sculptures including the school of stainless steel and aluminum dolphins which fly behind Florida's Capitol but the lions may be the most iconic. Go to Venice and you'll see winged lions everywhere. Our lions lack wings, but they have power, strength and majesty.

Nicholson was in his 70's when he created the lions. He lived on the West Coast near San Francisco, and passed away in 2008 at the age of 88, but we still have a piece of his vision in the middle of the Square, surrounded by the fountain. We are not alone. His art is displayed at MOMA, the Library of Congress, the Boston Museum of Fine Arts, and Le Bibliotheque Nationale de France in Paris.

Even the smallest corners of San Marco Square contain public art. The bike racks are made to replicate large bicycle chains topped by a rider on a touring bike. The gazebo is topped with lion faces around the crown. Everywhere you look in San Marco Square there is art--and don't forget to check out the sculptures in front of Theatre JAX and the San Marco Bookstore. Some might say that the facade of the bookstore itself, with its collection of book spines, is also a work of art. We would, anyway.

So that's a reason we love San Marco. We hope you'll check the art out, and enjoy it as we do.

Rob Smith - San Marco History, by Rob Smith

My wife and family moved to San Marco from Fort Myers. My late wife, Linda Larkin Smith, grew up in Murray Hill and Lakeshore. When we chose to return to Jacksonville she agreed, with some trepidation to buy a house in San Marco at the corner of Maple Lane and Laurel Road. Linda, our 7 year old son Bob, and I moved in August 1987.

Once in residence we were amazed at the welcome we received from our neighbors. In a short period of time we were included in many events. Several weeks before Christmas we were told by our new friends, Woody & Susan Fields, that they and several other couples were planning to stage a Nativity Scene in the Fields' front yard on Arbor Lane. This had not been done before in the neighborhood. The other primary instigators were the late Barbara Puckett, Judy Blumberg, and the Rink and Reynolds families. The participants wore robes borrowed from local churches. The small event received positive response – and was a whole lot of fun.

The following year the Nativity grew in interest and magnitude. An animal in the form of a goat borrowed from a neighbors' back yard was added. Men in the neighborhood were asked to stand in shifts on a Saturday or Sunday evening dressed either as a wise man or a shepherd. A teenage girl & boy played Mary & Joseph. There was a Cast Party for all participants held on Friday evening before the two night event. The event was entirely sponsored and financed by the Fields as a gift to the neighborhood.

In following years the Nativity event grew in interest, and attendance. Neighborhood men vied for selection to participate, with the job of wise man considered a major achievement. A carriage rental company was included that not only provided rides through the neighborhood, but also provided animals for free with a hefty tip. One of the animals - Bargain, the donkey - became a fast favorite. Sheep and calves were added to the mix. The animals were delivered on Saturday, and were our responsibility until Monday morning. A bunch of City guys taking care of the animals fostered many bizarre moments and a wealth of not so clean animal jokes.

One year, Bargain, the aforementioned Donkey, spent a Sunday night in the Fields back yard, and somehow got out. The Fields saw him walking out onto Arbor Lane early Sunday morning headed to Hendricks Ave. When two men went out to get him, Bargain decided to run – and did so to the railroad track off Marco Place – where he headed South. He was finally caught when he decided to stop running.

Bargain and several sheep spent time at our house. Rides were provided to children around and around and around my yard. Afterward, we had the greenest lawn in the neighborhood. That same year two very large and stubborn rams refused to walk the two blocks from my house to the Nativity. A neighborhood Great Dane was employed to no avail. Two men were assigned to each ram to pull and push them the two block route. We learned that being an animal keeper is hard work, but good exercise. And more animal jokes!

Another memorable Nativity occurred when the Shriners of Orlando advertised that they had a Camel that they would provide for events. So, four Shriners arrived in a converted school bus with a Camel hanging its head out of the rear window. The rest of the bus was well stocked with beer. Three of the Shriners were greatly enjoying the beer, and sharing it with the camel. He was handed a beer that he held in his mouth, bit the can and drained the contents. With this kind of entertainment and an afternoon to kill, it was decided that the Nativity robes would be donned and the Camel paraded through the neighborhood. The camel was a hit for the evenings Nativity. Around midnight the camel and three very drunk Shriners loaded up in the bus and their designated driver took off to the next day's event.

The Fields family ultimately moved on, and the Nativity became the responsibility of others. Today, 28 years later, through the determination of residents of San Marco, the

Nativity is still presented. Times and people have changed, but the anticipation of maybe getting to be a wise man, the prospect of entertaining children, and having a really great time with good friends and neighbors still persists. The event is now presented by the San Marco Preservation Society. The Nativity is just one of the many positive activities that are part of living in the San Marco Neighborhood.

Scott Summey - WHAT'S SO GREAT ABOUT SAN MARCO?

What's so great about living and working in a community like San Marco? So many things come to mind. Charming homes, friendly neighbors, loyal customers, and restaurants, movies and ice cream all within walking distance. Having lived in the San Marco area for nearly 18 years, it's really hard to imagine calling anywhere else home.

After buying a small two-story fixer upper on Felch Avenue in 1998, life got busy...getting married, adopting two crazy dogs and a cat, and rehabbing our first home. It was a fun and rewarding nine years. All the hard work and renovations paid off when we sold our house at the height of the housing boom. As a result, we were lucky enough to be able to purchase another fixer upper--our current residence on River Oaks Road.

Living life everyday as part of the San Marco community has been a wonderful experience. Seeing our friends pass by on foot or bike each day, walking dogs every night through lovely, tree-lined streets are just a couple of the things that make us thankful to live in such an ideal location.

Not only do we enjoy living in this neighborhood, we love working in San Marco as well. As one of the owners of Open Road Bicycles, located in the Miramar shopping plaza, we often see folks out riding bikes they purchased from our store. The local community has been an important part of our business. We so appreciate our friends and neighbors who support local businesses such as ours.

One of the reasons our neighborhood business has been so successful is simply because San Marco is such a great place to ride bicycles. You can leisurely roll along on two wheels through the quaint streets at dusk, smelling what's cooking on a nearby grill or see the glow of someone's backyard fire pit. Or, if you are more daring and competitive, you can venture out onto the new bike lanes up and down San Jose Boulevard. We often comment how nice it is that a great workout awaits just outside our front door.

Great food is also just steps away. We love going to eat at one of our many favorite restaurants in San Marco after a nice long bike ride. Or on lazier days, just strolling to San Marco square for lunch or dinner. We also love walking to the square to enjoy a good movie and tasty food at our favorite historic dine-in movie theatre. On special occasions we'll get some ice cream for the walk home.

There are so many things that make living and working in this neighborhood such a treat. Good people, good local shops and restaurants, nice shady streets for walking, running and riding are just a few favorites. As fall approaches and the temperatures cool, get out on your own two feet or two wheels and discover or remind yourself what is truly so great about this neighborhood we call San Marco.

Jeff Trippe – A Parent's Paradise

I am not sure when I first became aware that San Marco is significantly different from most other neighborhoods around Jacksonville. It must have been at a very early age, though, because most Southsiders had to drive through there in order to reach the Main Street Bridge and cross into downtown, and I recall riding with my father so that he could show me his new office. Also, when I was in high school, my friends and I would go to listen to bluegrass music at a place on San Marco Boulevard called Applejack's, now long defunct. We also wondered what it might be like to belly up to the bar with the real men we'd see ambling into the Town Pump, another joint that predated the area's renaissance. It wasn't until 1989, though that I moved to Riviera Street an easy stroll from where Worman's Bakery was situated. My young son and I would go there early on Saturdays for pastries and then while away the mornings down by the river or at Landon Park. He was small enough then that I could hoist him onto the lowest branch of the lush magnolia tree that grew near the park's edge, where he would sit and eat his cheese danish, king of all that he surveyed.

A few years later, our family grew. I married Laura, gained a stepson, had a daughter, and dwelt for eleven years on the other side of Hendricks Avenue, on Brookwood Road.

By far, though, my fondest memories of the old neighborhood are the languid hours I spent with my children doing nothing in particular in River Oaks Park. This marshy spate of rolling meadows, wild-grown trees, and sprays of daisies meanders along narrow Craig's Creek, but its effect on the senses is broad: it is like a walk through Old Florida. The tall herons practice their patient angling there even into the damp cold of December, the red-winged blackbirds return every spring to the awakening reeds, and in summer the box turtles, who might seem so sleepy on their sunny log, can drop like grenades into the water the very instant they sense your approach. One late summer evening, just at dusk, my daughter and I saw a four-foot alligator poised on the bank near the footbridge, a privilege that her brothers (once they were convinced it was really true) envied for years. For the kids, I suppose, the park was both a lesson on wildlife and an enticement to the imagination; on any given morning, we half-expected to come upon the remains of the campfire where Huck Finn and Jim had been sitting just a few minutes earlier with their bacon and coffee.

One of our silliest traditions was begun there, too, thanks to nature's wiles. On the hottest day of the hottest month of the hottest summer we'd ever endured, the kids and I were riding through the park on our bikes, sweating and griping, and as we approached the terminus of the creek where the St. Johns River finally opens up so suddenly that it is like falling off a cliff, one of the boys (I don't remember which one) made the decision to keep going, riding his two-wheeler straight into the river. There was nothing for the rest of us to do but follow, and then we were all wallowing in the cool water, with our astonished dog, Lucky, barking at us from the bank until she was convinced to come in as well.

We moved to Maine in 2006, and the kids are all grown up and gone now. I've learned to love New England, but I'll admit that on a winter's night, when I am in my little office upstairs and I hear the icy wind moaning in the pines, I sometimes wish to my soul that I could return to a searing summer's day in River Oaks Park, ride my bike straight toward

142

the delta of Craig's Creek, and hear the laughter of my children once again.

Philip Trippe – When I think of San Marco, I think of my youth. I think of my friends. I think of playing outside. I think of the St. Johns River. Most of all, I think "home." In a city with plenty of undesirable and even dangerous neighborhoods, I consider myself lucky to have grown up in such a charming, welcoming, and historic part of town. San Marco is a great place to raise a family, which is evidenced by the fact that most of the households *are* families. While there are certainly a few affluent neighborhoods in San Marco, with curvy streets lined by beautiful homes (which were usually the best neighborhoods to trick-or-treat in), they stop short of being pretentious like some of their First Coast counterparts. Despite everything it has going for it, San Marco still humbly holds on to the history and friendliness that makes it so special.

My first San Marco (and Jacksonville) residence was on Riviera Street, where I lived with my dad in the downstairs unit of a classic two story, brick San Marco home that had been converted into a duplex. Some of the earliest and fondest memories I have are of walking up the street to Worman's Bakery & Deli in the morning for a bite to eat. I'm sure I had other things to eat there, but the only thing I remember were the big cookies topped with icing that was ½ white and ½ black. It was at that house on Riviera Street where I can also recall my first snow, the Great Florida Blizzard of 1989. People had no idea what to do about the stuff, including my dad, who I can just barely remember ingeniously using a brick on the car windshield as an ice scraper. To his credit, who owns an actual ice scraper in Florida?

143

A few years later he bought a white house with my stepmom on Brookwood Rd., which was where I would spend half of the next 15 or so years. The other half was spent at my mom's, who around the same time moved up from Gainesville and bought an equally charming house on Flagler Ave, just 1.5 miles from my dad's. Both houses were part of the "San Marco Preservation Society", and both were great places to grow up.

Growing up in San Marco, I was fortunate to live within a short distance of a few friends. As an elementary school student at Hendricks Avenue, I would rollerblade or bike to the Foote's house (or the Feet, as we liked to affectionately call them) in the morning, where I would meet up with my good bud Joe and continue on to school from there. Joe and I were also baseball teammates year after year at HACAA, just up the road on Hendricks Ave. Of course for the majority of those years the league was called Hendricks Avenue Baptist, or HAB.

Eventually I got into skateboarding, as many of my friends did, and the elementary school I had once attended as a student became one of our favorite skate spots. We had many throughout San Marco, and countless hot, humid hours were spent pushing around the area on our boards, sweaty and flushed but always eager to ollie the next staircase or nose slide the next curb.

In 2004 I graduated from Episcopal High School, not far from San Marco, and went off to college in North Carolina. Since then the time that I've spent in San Marco has been few and far between, but it will always hold a special place in my heart. As I write this I'm struck with a longing to return to the ol' stomping grounds. Maybe I'll go back soon and watch the sunset over the St. Johns, get some pizza at The Loop, and catch a flick at the San Marco Theater. That sounds pretty perfect right about now.

Kim Walters – I love San Marco for so many reasons. From riding bikes with my daughter to the square for ice cream, walking to one of the many fabulous restaurant's on date night with my guy, or watching sunsets on the river with a fishing pole. We moved here so my daughter could go to Hendricks Elementary, we stay because there is no better place in Jacksonville. San Marco will always be home for us.

Cathy Watkiss – The Tree – Our Gift

It all began in 1989 when the San Marco Garden Circle voted to adopt the newly dedicated Gazebo in Balis Park as a Holiday Beautification Project. Our plans were to simply have a tall fresh cut Balsam Fir tree with hundreds of tiny white lights and hanging baskets of red poinsettias in place by December 4. Our budget was not to exceed $500.00. We embellished with yards of red velvet ribbons and banked the steps with more poinsettias and the fragrant narcissus, "paper whites", and sold them to shoppers passing through the park… it was the perfect fund raiser! The Garden Circle received a letter from the Preservation Society recognizing our efforts in beautifying the Square for the Holiday Season.

The following year we voted to continue The Tree Tradition. More members got involved and husbands pitched in a helping hand. We hauled ladders, power cords, hundreds of lights, more red velvet ribbons and bows, garlands along with homemade goodies and hot cider… "We were a force!" Our Circle decided to apply for an award with the Garden Club of Jacksonville. There were photos and articles written for the newspapers and we fully expected recognition with the award.

For a couple of years we would harvest the trees from a willing residence in the neighborhood who had that perfect overgrown Christmas tree just ready for removal from their yard. Some years we visited the local tree lots for a donation. In 1994, Wes Taylor of Oaklawn Cemetery, volunteered to donate, deliver, and set up a beautiful tree, which he did forever and always right on time for our workday!

Our very own San Marco Fire Department with John Sheldon got involved. We still rely on our wonderful firemen to help with the high jobs of securing the tree and hanging the big wreathes on top of the campanile. Our Garden Circle honored both men and their dedication to our cause with plaques and gifts of appreciation at a luncheon meeting we held at Epping Forrest.

Our Circle sold fresh garlands, wreathes, flowers, homemade soups and pickles we made in the downtown canning kitchen. The Preservation Society set up a table to sell memberships and luminary. Our fund raising chair announced "This is the beginning of great things to come in future years!" We made $2,000.00 that year under The Tree which we allocated to maintain our park projects in the neighborhood.

As each year became more festive, with "Magic on the Square", we began decorating earlier to accommodate all of the events planned. After our Circle took a vote, we reluctantly decided we needed a "faux tree". It was difficult to keep a live tree "lovingly water" for so many weeks and some Decembers were quite warm and hard on the live tree. We agreed but then, where to store it had to be considered. After being in a few garages, Zim Boulos offered to store the tree and all of the trimmings at the OE&S warehouse.

The Tree is a gathering place for the much anticipated Tree Lighting Ceremony which is usually the first Friday of December. Southside Baptist Church provides a wonderful sound system and seating for the event. The emcees are President of the San Marco Preservation Society, President of the San Marco Merchants Association, and our City Council Representative. Entertainment is provided by youth from local schools and church groups. Our longest standing entertainment comes from Hendricks Avenue Elementary School's 5th grade class Melody Makers and Recorder Group, LaVilla Performance Band, Southside United Methodist Children's Choir and teen guitar performers. The young and the older alike are full of excitement with the anticipation and arrival of Santa Claus and his Elves and it has become a popular backdrop for family photographs.

In the past 27 years, The Tree has been decorated with many new embellishments and seen many admiring faces.

Just as it was stated in December 1992…

"This is the beginning of great things to come in the future years as the San Marco Community continues to come together in celebration of a beautiful time of year and most importantly, it flourishes."

Sheri & Gary Webber – *It's the story of the boy and girl next door. They lived in Lakewood, went to church in San Marco, and attended school on the north end of US1/Phillips Highway. As two artsy teenagers wandering around San Marco Square*

147

in the mid-80s, they joked about which house they wanted to live in when they "grew up" and what kind of shop each would own if they could. It was the stuff of dreams. To think that Gary Webber, his wife Sheri, and their four teenage children now live in one of the very houses they swooned over, it seems like a fairytale. Be assured that it's real. Here's their story...

I can remember selecting the house at 1821 San Marco Place as a subject for one of my drawing projects while attending Jacksonville University in the early 90s. The much-older home sat regally on the corner in all of its white brick and green-shutter glory. A huge live oak dipped branches toward the bend in the road and it almost begged to be drawn. At the time, I had no idea what the future would hold, and neither did I realize what the past held regarding this historic home. I was there simply to record in charcoal and ink the slope of the roof and dappled lighting across the lawn, unaware that the home was once owned by a successful businessman who had the house replicated inch-for-inch after his own home in New England. Before he could convince his wife to leave the home she'd grown to love and move to the wilds of South Jacksonville in the late 1930s, he had to promise to 'bring the house.'

For Gary, San Marco was not only a popular arts destination for local youth, it was the stomping grounds for students attending Southside Baptist Church (SSBC). Soon it became a place where milestones happened. His siblings were baptized there, he and his fellow graduates were recognized there. Gary volunteered, sang, taught, and studied within its walls, feeling the welcoming and caring environment that hallmarks the 'church with the big white columns.'

In 1993, I walked the aisle of SSBC's sanctuary and married him—my high school sweetheart. Later that same decade, SSBC purchased #1821, along with two other homes adjacent to the main structure of the church, and in the early days of the new millennium, the parking lot that now services San Marco merchants and church members alike was constructed on San Marco Place. Little did I know that my youngest daughter, Maisy, would one day learn to ride without training wheels in that parking lot or that Gary's father, Larry Johnson, would hang a swing in the old live oak at #1821. In 1993, we were young and in love with our noses pointed toward Texas.

In 2001, our connection to San Marco and our home church deepened despite our absence. Gary's mother, Terry Lynn Johnson, passed unexpectedly in January of that year, leaving behind a very young, very large family who sorely felt her loss. A playground was built on San Marco Place and dedicated in her memory in 2002, a reminder of the woman who so thoroughly dedicated her life to the children of SSBC and San Marco. Over the many years that followed we continued to return home, finding Jacksonville and San Marco greatly changed. Ordinations, sibling weddings, baptisms, birthdays, and holidays were all celebrated at the corner of Hendricks and Atlantic.

Our family pulled back into San Marco with a semi, a minivan, four kids, and a dog in October of 2008. Gary had accepted SSBC's offer to return as senior pastor and help lead the church out of a difficult season of decline. He was a rookie pastor and I was a stay-at-home-mom, but both of us were determined to love on the church and community the way they loved on us for so many decades. More milestones have been reached since and added to the long list of San Marco moments, including Maisy's baptism, Emma and Caleb learning to drive, family portraits on the Square, Gary performing at Theatre Jacksonville, Abby serenading passersby with her violin, Caleb learning the chocolate business at Peterbrooke, Emma's and Maisy's days at Julia Landon College Preparatory, and many a family dinner at The Loop.

It has been a true privilege to live and serve in this historic, riverside community. In many ways, I feel as if San Marco helped shape us into the unique arts-loving, civic-minded, Christ-centered family that we are today. Nothing can replace the memories of my children sliding down the pole at Station #13 or Emma taking her senior prom photos at the Gazebo. Nothing can replace walking hand-in-hand to San Marco Theater to steal away by ourselves for a few hours, or walking the tree-lined streets. Watching the world from our screened porch, attending arts festivals, inhaling the drifting aroma of Maxwell House downtown, playing corn hole with friends down the street, and fetching newspapers for an older neighbor—these moments are priceless and never easy to quantify with words. We tease about 'getting kicked out of San Marco' because our teenagers are too loud and we have too many weeds in the yard. But truth be told, we hope to never leave.

Jan White – I never imagined the adventures that awaited me when I brought two sons into the world! My first memories of the San Marco area include the Easter Hat Parade as my boys attended South Jacksonville Presbyterian Preschool and, of course, Mims Bakery…sitting on stools at the counter enjoying countless delicious breakfasts after dropping the boys off! And as they grew and decided to join Cub Scouts, I was right there as Den Mother and later, when they "graduated" into Boy

Scout Troop 35, I actively participated as a committee member and later as an Assistant Scoutmaster. That was a time, mind you, when there were not many (if any) female leaders that were willing to get down in the dirt, camping, hiking, canoeing with a bunch of pre-teen to teen-aged boys….and love it! But love it, I did. It wasn't long after my own boys aged out at 18 years old, that I became Scoutmaster (by default!) as no other dads were rushing in to volunteer, and there were at least 20 boys who desperately wanted to work through the ranks and experience the fun of scouting. So, after a few raised eyebrows and serious meetings with those who were not sure this was the place for a woman to serve, several supporters encouraged me to not let the doubters give me the boot, and for the next 14 years I served as Scoutmaster, which turned out to be the best years ever! Putting the scouts through proper training and then stepping back to watch them grow and develop leadership skills was truly rewarding. Then seeing them put it all together as we embarked on numerous camping and high-adventure backpacking trips made it all worth the effort. Along the way we gathered some awesome dads that did serve with me as assistant scoutmasters, and have become life-long friends that were so appreciated. Some of my favorite times were cold nights around a blazing campfire listening to the boys talk about just about anything and everything! I was treated just like "one of the guys", with respect of course; at least up until the day we stood at the top of Devil's Courthouse attempting our very first repelling adventure. After getting all our gear on and listening to the guides who were with us explain how to go about dropping over the rock's edge, I experienced, for the first time ever, a unanimous "ladies first!". I was not prepared for that, wanting to watch a few others do this before my attempt occurred, but what choice did I have? They were being such gentlemen! That was probably the first of many, many thrills that being their Scoutmaster gave me the opportunity to experience – Backpacking in New Mexico at Philmont, canoeing the boundary waters in Canada, snorkeling and sailing at Sea Base in the Keys and many other memorable camping trips right here in our area. The troop grew from 20 to 55 boys during the 14 years I spent with them and I wouldn't trade those days for anything! I now serve as the Riverbend District Advancement Chairman and still have the pleasure of working with Eagle candidates in the district, who have provided countless Eagle projects to enhance and improve our San Marco community, including the scouts in Troop 35!

Mark O. Wilbanks – Transition. Revitalization. Two words that come to mind when I think about the 90s. San Marco was on the way back. So was the church I served, Southside Baptist. Present in the community since 1939, Southside was experiencing a resurgence as a congregation and as a member of the community. The fellowship began to grow with the addition of young adults and families. In a renovation/construction project, the church doubled in facility size with space that could be utilized by both church and community.

The church also strengthened its ties with other churches in the San Marco/San Jose area to offer seasonal community worship services and to contribute to United Community Outreach Services (UCOM). The Trotter Activities Center became the home for Biddy Basketball, a well-known program for elementary ages.

One of Southside's most enjoyable community events that we liked to call a "Jacksonville Tradition" was the Singing Christmas Tree that provided an annual introduction to the

Christmas season. Multiple performances each year helped our community get in the spirit of the season.

Early in our ministry there, I took a walking tour around San Marco. Stopping several people on the street, I asked if they knew where Southside Baptist Church was located. A few people pointed to the big white church on the corner of Hendricks and Atlantic. I'll never forget what one man said. He remarked, "It's right over there, but it wouldn't matter if it was there or not." We were determined to prove otherwise. Southside was proud to be a positive influence for the people of San Marco and beyond.

Jeanette Yates – For many communities around the country, fall season is signaled by a crisp chill in the air or the changing colors of leaves. For the people of San Marco however, fall is here with the pumpkins arrive on the front lawn at Southside United Methodist Church. Each year during the first October weekend, a large truck backs up onto "The Point" and thus the unloading begins. One by one, the pumpkins are transported from the back of the truck to the palates spread throughout the Patch. A "Bucket Brigade" style line of volunteers work in seamless rhythm moving thousands of pumpkins, arranging them in rows upon rows. SUMC members of all ages and even some friendly neighbors come out for this event that though it is hard work, ends up being a time of laughter and fun.

The SUMC Pumpkin Patch was started about 20 years ago to raise funds for mission and outreach initiatives of the church. Today, youth workers and their families volunteer time and the proceeds are placed in a fund to help those students participate in mission work both locally and internationally. However, to say that the Pumpkin Patch is just

153

another church fundraiser, would be missing the real point all together- The Pumpkin Patch is a San Marco landmark.

Once the big truck pulls away after the unloading, the Patch officially opens and the San Marco community begins planning their annual trek to the SUMC Pumpkin Patch. For some, like our local teachers, it's time to plan a storytelling time-something arranged through the church-where children walk, or are brought by bus or van, to hear a story in the patch, sitting among the pumpkins, and perhaps even get to take home a 'spooky'- teeny pumpkins just the right size for little hands. For others, after seeing that the Pumpkin Patch has been set up, outfits are chosen and family photo shoots planned- a yearly tradition much cherished. Sometimes special events are held at SUMC like the Annual Fall Festival or Trunk or Treat. These, too, are much held traditions of San Marco residents.

This landmark, The Southside United Methodist Church Pumpkin Patch, is unique in that it is only present one month a year. But in the hearts, and photo albums, of San Marco families, it is a reminder of community and tradition.

Officer Glen Youngblood - Remember a time when neighbors and shop owners knew each other and community ties were strong?

Where you could just walk from home to your church, diner, coffee shop, movie house or fire station.

Those "Good Ole Days" are not forgotten in an area of Jacksonville known as San Marco.

History is alive and well here as I stand in the gazebo at

Balis Park in the center of what I refer to as a modern-day "Mayberry".

The Southside Baptist church bells ring for the noon hour followed by a bell hymn of praise, thanks to their restoration benefactors Bob and Virginia Ivey. Eager customers quickly fill the satisfying restaurants and stores for the lunch hour. A "Walking Beat" officer sees every side of an area and meets the most interesting and unusual folks, from the business owners, workers and politicians to the mailman and the occasional misbehaver. San Marco becomes a part of us and we are a part of San Marco. There is a strong sense of family unity and belonging here that stretches across time itself. I am not sure whether "Sheriff Andy Taylor" or "Deputy Barney Fife" is more applicable, but the people of San Marco treat me like family and the sentiment is shared. We want the best for our family and we protect each other in Our Neighborhood. Visitors from around the world as well as our regular city travelers often stop to ask the police officer for directions or advice on where to eat or enjoy their time in the city. I always smile and say, "You've come to the right place, we have everything you need." I do have to ask what their preferences are because we have so many choices. One traveler laughed and responded, "Well I knew I was asking the right person," as I shared my list of favorites. Today I made my way around the square on the sidewalk when I noticed a couple of little faces looking up at me from a table where they were enjoying a hot pizza with mom. The family dog was at their feet enjoying a cool bowl of water and sniffing for the pizza. I asked if they knew anyone who liked police stickers, holding up a sticker for each. They both got excited and gladly took one as I explained that they had to help me by doing exactly what their mom asked and by staying out of trouble all day. There was a brief moment of silence as they looked at Mom and then back at me. Mom smiled too as she broke the silence, "It's a deal!" I told them to have a great day and I continued my tour around the block. I checked in with my business owners, trading hellos and waves as I met Forrest Brewer at the Wardroom; he always has the scoop. He relayed everything I may have missed over the weekend and he shared an historical lesson for the area that, once again, confirmed how long he has been paying attention to San Marco. Somer from Leila's dress shop stopped in and she offered to pick up lunch for Forrest and Patty since she was headed to the Beach's Diner. They declined and thanked her as Patty held up a cup of sweet tea, indicating that she already made a trip herself. My radio let out a loud alert tone and broke the moment because there was a traffic crash nearby. The rescue unit and fire truck from station 13 had apparently received the same information as they begin loading up too. I jogged back to my police car and we became a parade of lights and sirens on Atlantic Boulevard to Hendricks Avenue making our way to the crash. Traffic and pedestrians alike paused at the stir of activity, but they quickly returned to their destinations as we left the Square. After directing traffic and clearing vehicles from the crash, it was time to pay a visit to my friends at Peterbrooke where the coconut gelato hits the spot on a hot day. It's a good thing they call it a Walking Beat. Just as I entered the door and took a deep breath of Chocolate, my phone rang and Michele at the Marble Slab told me that a suspicious person and a car were nearby. I quickly made my way across the street and through the alley but the people were already gone. I wasn't too disappointed though because this is where you can enjoy a frosty Swiss Mocha ice cream while discussing crime prevention tips with Michelle's husband Gerry. Some days are almost perfect, where the scarecrow of a blue suit and a police car do exactly what they were meant to, even if it doesn't always dissuade an occasional "Otis" who is standing in the

Lion's Fountain, fishing out spare change, but it's still a ride whether he or she chooses to leave peacefully or they spend a night in Sheriff Taylor's Jail.

Just in case you were wondering, Aunt Bea will not be bringing them dinner, but I will whistle a toon all the way home.

See you all tomorrow.

Esher Yu, 5th grade – I think Hendricks Avenue Elementary makes San Marco special and unique because at this school kids are kind. Also, teachers here care and love their students. They are very kind and encouraging. We also connect with our community through things like the walkathon, which is when we have business partners who donate money and like half of the school or more come out to participate and help raise money.

I have enjoyed this school a lot since I moved here in the 3rd grade and I have found great friends, amazing teachers, and a wonderful Principal and Vice-Principal.

We also have fun after school activities at our school such as, chess, 5th grade chorus, 5th grade ambassadors, melody makers, drama club, science club and sketch club. We have resources such as computer lab, media, P.E., music, recess, and much more. We also have gifted classes with two amazing teachers, Mrs. Seeker, and Ms. Pearthree.

A lot of kids walk to school, or ride a bike, which helps the environment because it doesn't cause air pollution. Each kid has their own special personality unique to our school and community.

That is why I think Hendricks Avenue Elementary helps make San Marco special and unique.

Seaman Zimmerman - My *memories* of San Marco go back about sixty-five years from the time I was about 5 years old. I have lived at the same address for nearly seventy years. I remember playing in our yard when I was a toddler or going to FEC Park which was behind our home to play with my siblings or with our dog. I remember the old steam locomotives that used to pull some of the FEC freight trains. The Landon football team coached by Barney Searcy used to practice in the park. Neighborhood children including me would play football or baseball in pick-up games in the park. We traveled by bikes, roller skated, walked and even played in the streets because traffic was not a problem. Hendricks Avenue was a two lane street in the early years of my life. Growing up, our homes never were locked because it seemed like everyone knew everyone in the neighborhood and looked out for each other. I remember when consolidation came to Jacksonville and the city limits exploded and we became the "Bold New City of the South".

Many of us went first to Southside Grammar and then to Landon for our public education in classrooms that were not air conditioned. Lasting friendships were developed and many professionals in Jacksonville are still part of the community and are active in many of the local charities. I remember the good times in "The Square" at the bowling alley or just walking around at the stores including A & P and Setzer's grocery stores, the two pharmacies, the three gas stations,

Mim's Bakery, the "Dime Store" and the little shops that sold clothes. I remember the old tennis courts, swimming pool, and the public library on Hendricks Avenue next to Post 88. I also remember going to the park at the river end of River Oaks Road and fishing or sometimes watching some of the little boats come into the creek from the St. Johns River. I remember the old Oriental Gardens which was just a short distance from where I grew up. I remember how the neighborhood was loaded with children when I was young and as the families matured I remember the neighborhood changing to almost no children for about 25 years.

I have seen the revival in the neighborhood with families moving in and children once again playing every day. Most of all, I remember the convenience of living in San Marco, the ease of getting around Jacksonville, and the friendliness of the residents in San Marco.

Churches

All Saints Episcopal Church – 4171 Hendricks Avenue

November 7, 2010 marked a milestone in the life of All Saints Episcopal Church. On this day, All Saints Sunday, our parish concluded a year-long celebration of Christian ministry from 1885-2010. With the theme of "125 Years of Ministry: Gratitude, Service, Trust," we looked back on our past thankful for the faith, vision, and service of our forbearers - both in the distant past and in our parish now. In 1885, a small gathering of Episcopalians answered the call to found an Episcopal presence in South Jacksonville. They first met in the shared terminal waiting room of the Jacksonville, St. Augustine and Halifax River Railway and the St. John's Ferry. Five years later and with many more parishioners, a church was built further south on Hendricks Avenue, where the Florida Baptist Convention state offices are now located. Church membership continued to grow and the congregation moved to the present location of All Saints. The move offered an opportunity to build a larger facility that could function as a church and parish hall, with an adjoining Christian education building. The present church building was consecrated in 1965, the nursery was filled, and the church office was busy with activity. The pace has not slowed down. Our ministries range from a renowned lay ministry and counseling center, a five-star inter-generational daycare center, numerous missions ministries for the underserved homeless and hungry, two Sunday and two mid-week worship services, Bible studies, adult Christian education and Sunday school. All Saints is a thriving fellowship of Christians who endeavor to answer Christ's call "to love God with all out heart, soul, mind and strength and our neighbors as ourselves."

Source: www.allsaintsjax.org

Assumption Catholic Church – 2431 Atlantic Blvd

It was in the early autumn of the year 1913 that the prayers of a small group of Catholic laity in South Jacksonville were answered, when His Excellency, The Most Reverend William J. Kenny established the parish of the Assumption on the south shores of the St. John's River. The parish of about 140 members attended the first Mass in a rented store in Oct 5 1913. Father Patrick Frank Barry lived above the store. Within a year with the help of the Catholic Extension Society and Mr. Wm. Byrne a church and rectory were built on Gary Street (formerly Catherine St.) where the Jacksonville expressway now passes.

In October 1917 Father Barry was appointed Vicar General of the diocese. Father Patrick J. Bresnahan came from the missions of West Florida and took over the newly built church on Gary Street. There was considerable growth in the parish resulting from the arrival of many catholic families from the north after WWI.

In 1923 a contract was signed to start construction of a new parish hall and school. The school opened that fall with an enrollment of 110 students. The school was staffed with four Sisters of St. Joseph from St. Augustine. Sister Mary Agnita was the first principal.

In 1924, ill health overtook Father Bresnahan and he was succeeded by Reverend Father Malachy F. Monahan. Father Monahan, a native of Ireland, served at Immaculate

Conception and St. Monica in Palatka. His arrival was at the beginning of a period when financial difficulties assailed the parish, but none the less continued to grow in spite of the Depression. Valuable assistance came from the members of the Holy Name Society, the Children of Mary, the Altar and Rosary Society and other parish groups. The first meeting of the Assumption Guild, held in April 1937 was presided over by Father Monahan, who for many years served as Chaplin of Bishop Kenny Council of the Knights of Columbus.

Father George Rockett, (later to become Msgr. Rockett) succeeded as pastor in the war clouded year of 1942. Plans for the expansion were postponed until the end of WWII, and in 1945 Father Rockett began investigating the possibility of acquiring a parcel of land known as the "Locarno Tract." This property on Atlantic Blvd was finally acquired by the Diocese through his successor, Msgr James B. Cloonan at a time of growth in the Southside area.

Father Cloonan's service to the Church in Florida spanned more than 30 yrs. He served in Miami Beach, Homestead, Fort Meyers and Palm Beach before he entered the armed forces during WWII as a chaplain. From 1944-47 Father Cloonan served with the rank of Major in the Pacific area. It was at the termination of his service that he came to serve at Assumption. He presided over unprecedented growth which Jacksonville experienced in the post war years. He was confronted at once with the need to expand the parish's facilities.

Father Cloonan's first project was to convert the existing building into a temporary school and convent on the original site of Fort St. Nicholas. That existing building was designed by famed architect, Henry John Klutho, in 1909. It was once a Merrill-Stevens office building, once the Gibbs ship building company during WWI, and once a sewing factory. The new Assumption School opened in September of 1949 with an enrollment of 317 students. The school also saw a change in the Order of Sisters that were teaching in the school. The St. Joseph nuns left and eight Sisters of St. Dominic of Adrian Michigan arrived to staff the school. Sister Marie Joseph Barry, niece of the founding pastor, was the first Dominican principal.

The year 1950 was one of special significance for Assumption Parish. On November 1st of that year His Holiness Pope Pius XII of venerable memory defined the dogma of the Assumption of the Blessed Virgin Mary. Since ours is the only Church of the Assumption in the Diocese of St. Augustine, it was chosen as the site for a Pontifical High Mass offered by His Excellency, the Most Reverend Thomas J. McDonough, Auxiliary Bishop of St. Augustine, to mark the occasion.

Under Father Cloonan, a new church building was built on the site of the school in 1955 when the city acquired the original property (old Church and buildings) for the Jacksonville Expressway. The present Church was dedicated by Archbishop Joseph P. Hurley. Also in this year Father Cloonan was elevated to the rank of Monsignor. A new rectory and convent were built in 1956 and 1958 respectively. Msgr. Cloonan died in November 1963 which happened to be the year of our 50th anniversary. Celebration for the golden jubilee was postponed until April 1964.

As enrollment increased, so did the need for more space. In 1965 an additional school building and a parish hall were built under the guidelines of Monsignor Harold Jordan. This addition made available eight more classrooms. The auditorium in the school was renovated to house the school library. Our Lady's Chapel was dedicated by the Bishop on

June 16, 1973. The bell tower was added in 1974 to the back of Our Lady's Chapel. Msgr Jordan went to the Cathedral in St. Augustine as Rector in June 1977.

Monsignor Eugene Kohls, pastor from 1977 to 2002, served the longest of its eight pastors so far. He oversaw the interior remodel of the original school building and constructed a meeting hall now named after him. A pre-school was begun in the downstairs of the former convent.

Reverend Frederick Parke, formerly from St Elizabeth Ann Seton in Palm Coast, FL became pastor in 2002. By securing the funds and finalizing the design he completed the Rosary Garden. He soon began the Heritage and Horizons program to remodel the school courtyard followed by the construction of the Family Center Gymnasium and meeting room building. At the same time the ministry of Perpetual Adoration began which brought about Christ Renews His Parish, the Servant Sisters of Home of the Mother, many vocations to the priesthood and the religious life. Finally the complete renovation and redecoration of our church, including the addition of St. Joseph's Chapel, Divine Mercy Chapel, and the Tower Garden. Adoration has been the singular blessing to Assumption which has brought about many more blessings. The next phase of Heritage and Horizons will be the new Early Childhood Learning Center which will house the Kindergartens, Pre-School and Child Care programs.

Our Centennial year began October 2012. This memorable year was celebrated with many events such as the Parish Family Campout, Historical Church Tour, Alumni Celebration Dance, and Wedding Vow Renewal.

Source: www.assumptioncatholicchurch.org

City Church – Landon Middle School 1819 Thacker Ave

Pastor Blake Bennett 2015 – Present

TheCity.church, a new life-giving church centrally located near downtown. Before planting TheCity.church, Blake served as Executive Director of YouthQuake Live, a Jacksonville based youth movement that impacts thousands of students with its monthly shows.

Source: thecity.church

Hendricks Avenue Baptist Church – 4001 Hendricks Avenue

Pastor: Kyle Reese

1945 – Hendricks Avenue Baptist Church meets in the Little Theater in San Marco, renting the facility for $25 per Sunday, with Pastor Warren Walker, Deacons are Terry Parker, Fred Darby, Melvin Hill, and W.K. Hatcher. There are 48 names on the original church register. Later that year, 14 acres of land is purchased on Hendricks Avenue. Ground is broken for a multi-purpose building (gymnasium-fellowship hall-sanctuary). Choosing to build a gym with its very first bricks and mortar, underscores HAB's belief in recreation ministry from the very beginning.

1946 – Dr. C.M. Coalson is called as Pastor and the first worship service is held in the new facility.

1947 – Mary Thalleen becomes part-time minister of music.

1952 – Dr. O.E. Burton becomes Pastor.

1953 – Dr. Clyde B. Lipscomb becomes Pastor.

1958 – The new sanctuary is finished. Gertrude Welch becomes church organist

1962 – Two Educational Wings are built.

1965 – Mickey King becomes Minister of Youth & Recreation Director.

1968 – Two more educational wings are built.

1975 – The Chapel is built.

1979 – Dr. Clyde Lipscomb retires as pastor of HAB after 26 years; he becomes Pastor Emeritus until his death in 1992.

1980 – Dr. Jack A. Snell becomes Pastor.

1985 – The first annual Palm Sunday "Blessing of the Palms" takes place, a joint celebration of HAB and its neighbors, All Saints Episcopal Church and St. Mark's Lutheran Church.

1996 – The HAB recreation program is changed to Hendricks Avenue Community Athletic Association (HACAA), a non-church owned activity controlled by a board of directors, so that the program can receive funds and support from the City Recreation Department.

1988 – Fellowship Hall is built.

1996 – HAB Celebrates 50 years.

2000 – The renovated Sanctuary is dedicated… Also dedicated is the new stained glass window, designed by world renowned stained glass artist, Paul Pickel of Vero Beach, Florida. The window depicts Christ with open arms, as well as several ministries specific to HAB. It is the largest such window in Florida. Dr. Snell retires after serving 20 years as Senior Pastor.

2002 – W. Gregory Pope becomes Sr. Pastor

September 24, 2006 – HAB celebrates its 60th anniversary; Dr. Kyle Reese is installed with blessings by Jack Snell and Greg Pope.

December 23, 2007 – A fire completely destroys the Sanctuary.

December 23, 2009 – New Sanctuary is opened!

Source: Laraine Humbert, HAB.

Jerusalem Missionary Baptist Church – 2010 Westmont St.

Pastor: Brian Campbell

The Early Years- 1872-1915:

As early as 1872, a minister of the Missionary Baptist Church preached the gospel throughout Jacksonville and saw the need of a church in the southern section of the city. With the Lord guiding him, Reverend Landsbury and a group of faithful believers officially organized Jerusalem Missionary Baptist Church on October 29, 1872. This church was located on Jerusalem Street.

168

From 1872 through 1915 the church saw a steady growth in its membership. Reverend Landsbury served several years before resigning. He was succeeded by Reverend William Payton who was followed by Reverend Goodson. Six years chronicles the ministry of Reverend G. H. Norman, who served as Jerusalem's fourth pastor. Henry Jackson was called as pastor after Reverend Norman. The church experienced a strong, spiritual growth during the time he served. Reverend Jackson resigned in 1915.

1916-1958:
In 1916 Reverend Solomon Cooper was called as pastor. The Deacon board consisted of Deacon John Henry and Deacon William Brown. Under the leadership of Reverend Cooper, the church auditorium was remodeled and the Educational Building was erected. During the forty two years he served as pastor, many people were baptized and added to the church membership. With new members and workers in the church, many worship programs and activities were added during this time of spiritual growth for the Jerusalem church family. Because of failing health, Reverend Cooper resigned in April of 1958. The assistant pastor, Reverend Jake Ray, served faithfully as Interim Pastor for the remainder of 1958.

1959-1992:
Reverend Richard W. Jackson was called as pastor of the church on January 22, 1959, and he took charge officially the first Sunday in February of that year. Under the divine guidance of the lord and the leadership of Reverend Jackson, the church was greatly blessed. The grounds, courtyard, and parking lots were upgraded.

Many souls were added to the church by baptism and restoration. Under his administration, five new deacons were added to the Deacon Board; with one deacon called into the Ministry. Two wards and a third choir were organized, and a church bus was purchased.

In March 1964, the congregation purchased property and erected the present church on the site where it now stands. The church was completed and dedicated under the leadership of Reverend Jackson.

During 1967, the church's mortgage was lifted from all church properties. The Educational Building and parking lot were completed, a new organ was purchased and the existing Sunday school complex was constructed, and dedicated on March 12, 1978.

During 1983, The R. W. Jackson Ensemble and Male Chorus were organized and were inspirational to the church. Reverend Robert Herring was ordained by Reverend Jackson in 1983, and he served for four years. In 1984, the Lord wonderfully blessed Jerusalem with two uplifting Associate Ministers, Reverend James A. Brown and Reverend Adolphus Lawrence. In July 1985, a business complex and double car garage were completed and dedicated. In 1992 a new church van was purchased. The Lord wonderfully blessed Jerusalem during the leadership of Reverend Jackson. After the retirement of Reverend Jackson on December 31, 1992, Reverend Randy Hezekiah served as Interim Pastor from February 7, through September 30, 1993.

1993-2001:
Reverend Johnny McKinnie was called as pastor on October 10, 1993. Many members were added to the church by conversion, letters and restoration. Under Reverend McKinnie's leadership, several improvements were made to

170

the church buildings. The Pastor's Study was remodeled; a new roof was added to the Educational Building, Fellowship Hall and Pastor's Study. In addition, new carpet was installed in the church sanctuary in May 1997. To further promote the spiritual growth of the church, new classes, choirs, and ministries were implemented during this time also.

In addition Jerusalem is now joined with the Emanuel Baptist Association, the Florida General Baptist State Convention and The National Baptist Convention USA Inc. In November 1996, the church became incorporated with the state of Florida, and is known as Jerusalem Missionary Baptist Church, Inc. As God continued to bless the spiritual growth of the church, Pastor McKinnie saw the need to add a part-time secretary to the staff. In February 1997, the position was filled. The secretarial office was completed and equipped with a computer and other necessary equipment.

Training for The Evangelistic Ministry began in March 1997 prior to implementing the Outreach Ministry. In 1997, six evangelistic teams began field work throughout the community.

In January 1998, another vision was realized with the implementation of the Married Couples and Women Fellowship Ministries. In April of that year, lighting improvements were made in the sanctuary and Fellowship Hall, and the Voices of Praise Chorale began singing to the glory of God.

In 1999 God continued to bless the church with the installation of an audio system in the Fellowship Hall and improvements were made to the system inside the sanctuary. A privacy gate was added to the parking lot, as well as an irrigation system. During this same year, Brother Marvin Mobley was licensed as minister of the Gospel. Classroom floors were replaced with tile and emergency lighting system were installed. In March of 2000, the Youth Ministry held their first bible study meeting.

In October 2001, the Lord led Reverend McKinnie to another church and congregation. During this transition, Jerusalem was under the leadership of the Board of Deacons for seventeen months.

2003-Present

On March 6, 2003, God placed our current Pastor, Reverend Brian C. Campbell, as the under-shepherd of this church. Pastor Campbell is a visionary who loves and cares for his congregation. Under Pastor Campbell's leadership, with the aid of the Holy Spirit, many souls have been added to the church. New Deacons have been ordained, and several ministries have been formed or renewed. Pastor Campbell has over seen the completion of several major church projects, such as; the underpinning stabilization project, repair of drainage pipelines in the fellowship hall and the Sunday school building. The sound system has been upgraded; music equipment has been replaced. Extensive repairs to church rental property and replacement of building signs on both sides of the church have also been completed under Pastor Campbell's leadership. An audio sound room has been added also.

In 2004, The Young At Heart Ministry was organized for senior members to unite and fellowship among each other, being able to feel the presence of the Lord. The Men's Ministry was also organized in 2004 through the divine guidance of our pastor. They thank God for their spiritual and social fellowship.

In 2007, a Thursday morning fellowship was established for our senior members. We have designated Thursday mornings for all seniors in our church and community to engage in a range of fun related activities including beach outings, fishing, bowling, movies and computers.

In August 2009 the church was blessed to see the beginning of construction on the new sanctuary. Our construction project was completed and we entered our new sanctuary May 2, 2010 to the Glory of God.

Source: www.jmbcjax.org

South Jacksonville Presbyterian – 2137 Hendricks Avenue

Ministers:

Bruce Hedgpeth	2016- Present
Stephen C Kolderup	2014-2016
Susan Takis	2004-2012 (Assoc)
Vincent C Kolb	2001-2014
Stephen Hulsey	1999-2001
Gary Eller	1998-1999
Kimberly Hyatt	1996-2000 (Assoc)
Kevin Pound	1993-1995 (Assoc)
John Kleinheksel	1991-1997 (Assoc)
David Stoker	1990-1997
Robert S Smith	1983-1990
Robert Fulton	1972-1974
Dr. Harvin	1959-Ret. 6/1970

South Jacksonville Presbyterian Church was an important part of Jacksonville's expansion south of the St.

Johns River in the early 1900's. The church is named for South Jacksonville, which was a separate town in 1913 when SJPC was established.

The church first began as a small Sunday school and as an outreach of First Presbyterian Church downtown. It held its meetings in a rented building not far from the river ferry that joined South Jacksonville with Jacksonville. Eventually, a small church was erected on the corner of LaSalle and Hendricks Avenue.

The first vehicular bridge over the St. Johns was completed in 1921, and South Jacksonville became a part of Jacksonville within a few years. Much of the original San Marco area was constructed during the 1920's and 1930's, resulting in the attractive residential areas and town square next to our sanctuary.

In 1937, Dr. Stephen T. Harvin moved from North Carolina to become SJPC's pastor. He wanted a new church and led the congregation in a mood of "building fever". In 1939, the same year as the New York World's Fair and the release of "Gone with the Wind" and "The Wizard of Oz" the church moved to the three story brick building first erected at its present location. During the 1940s, church membership grew dramatically, so much that the church had to rent a city bus to accommodate the men's Sunday school class that had to meet under the big oak tree in the yard.

In 1949, the congregation of around 1,000 members broke ground for a beautiful new church building and sanctuary. The first services were held in the new sanctuary in

1950. The church was a neighborhood center of worship and fellowship during those times, with bustling Sunday services, youth and choir programs, church circles, and fellowship and mission activities. By 1956, there were over 1,600 members with 1,000 enrolled in Sunday school. Soon the church began to broadcast its services on television. Over the years, a prayer chapel was built and additional property purchased, part of which became SJPC's Family Life Center.

Following Dr. Harvin's retirement in 1970, SJPC has been blessed with the leadership several wonderful pastors and associate pastors. In the years approaching the twenty-first century, SJPC membership dropped from its 1950s and 1960's high to under 1,000. This smaller more comfortable size has been a benefit in allowing members to know one another better and work together more closely.

Like most Americans, the congregation senses that life has changed forever over the last few years. In a world like this, SJPC provides answers and an anchor. The church proclaims that Jesus Christ is Lord and Savior even in the darkest and most confusing times. It keeps its eye on its purpose of telling the good news of salvation and acting as Christ's faithful evangelist in worship, education, fellowship, prayer, care and mission. The church looks forward to being a place of importance in the community, the nation and the world for a long time to come.

Source: www.sjaxpc.com

Southside Assembly of God – 2118 Kings Avenue

Senior Pastors:
Milton and Wanda Dykes

A revival held by Raymond T. Richey in 1924 brought together a group of people in the Billy Sunday Tabernacle on Liberty Street. After several years of revival, this group of people called Reverend E.R. Sanders to be their pastor. During the years that followed, the congregation met in buildings on 10th Street and Phelps and Liberty. In 1934 Pastor Fred Richey to over the church until 1937, when Reverend Ted Smith became pastor. In 1938, Clifford Knopf took over the leadership. During this time, the church met in the Naugle Funeral Home on Hendricks Avenue.

In 1941, with the installation of Pastor E.G. Lain, the church set up residence at 1227 Liberty Street. During this time, and the time that followed, the church was known as a Gospel Center and was non-denominational. It remained there until 1943, when it was decided that the church would re-locate to the Southside of town. William Horace Ricketson helped find the location. The Setzer's Bakery building at 809 Flagler Avenue was purchased and the meetings where conducted on the second floor in the "Upper Room."

In 1946, under Pastor Norman McCutchen, the church voted to join the Assemblies of God. In September of 1946, the church incorporated as Gospel Center. The church's first radio broadcasts occurred at this time on WOBS. It was the first Pentecostal broadcast in the Jacksonville area.

In 1949, the church changed the name of the charter with the city to Southside Assembly of God. Even so, the name used at that time, "Faith Tabernacle" continued to be used for many years. A new auditorium was built onto the front of the old bakery that year.

In 1952, the property at 1842 Olevia Street was purchased and a tent was erected for services until a building could be constructed.

1961 – J.B. Davis became pastor

1966, Dale C. Zink became pastor. The church held a city-wide crusade with Jimmy Swaggart. During this meeting, the church saw largest crowds in its history with attendance of nearly 750 people.

Fall of 1975 – record attendance of over 1,600

1976, Purchase of the Volkswagen dealership property on Kings Road to build a new Sanctuary. Dr. James D. Brown was Pastor at this time.

1978 – Pastor Paul D. Zink, developed a Television Ministry.

1982 – Pastor Stanley Lyon

1983 – Pastor Frank C. Mays

2002 – Present, Pastor Milton Dykes.

Source: Southside Assembly of God

Southside Baptist Church – 1435 Atlantic Blvd.

Pastors:
Dr. Gary Webber
Southwestern Seminary/ Beeson Divinity School
October. 2008- Present

Dr. R. Wayne Stacy
Southern Seminary
April 2004 - April 2007

Dr. Mark O. Wilbanks
Southern Seminary and New Orleans Seminary
September, 1985-June, 2002

Rev. Cornelius B. Davis
Southern Seminary
January, 1978 - January, 1984

Dr. Malcolm B. Knight
Southern Seminary
June, 1950-June, 1977

Rev. A. M. Herrington
Southwestern
October, 1945-October, 1949

Dr. W. Herschel Ford
Southwestern
July, 1939- July, 1945

On January 2, 1939, Southside Baptist Church was organized. It began, not as a mission, but by the merging of two small churches that had been established in South

Jacksonville. One of these churches, the First Baptist Church of South Jacksonville, had begun as a mission Sunday School of First Baptist Church, Jacksonville, as early as 1908. When its small building was erected, it was on the corner of Kipp Avenue and Louisa Street.

The other Church, the San Marco Boulevard Baptist Church, was organized in 1938. It met in the San Marco Theatre.

Leaders of the two churches, Dr. Solomon and Dr. Theodore Otto, decided to merge the congregations and build one great church. Southside Church had 419 members when organized. Dr. Otto served as supply pastor for six months. On July 1, 1939, Dr. W. Herschel Ford became the first pastor of the new church and served until 1945. The new church was meeting in the Kipp Avenue building. Under Dr. Ford's ministry the present strategic location on Atlantic Blvd and Hendricks Ave was acquired. The first unit, which constitutes our oldest educational building, was occupied Easter Sunday, March 24, 1940, with 589 in Sunday school.

In 1943 the church organized the Larsen Baptist Mission.

In the fall of 1945, the Reverend A.M. Herrington came from serving as a Chaplain in WWII to lead the church. He served for four years, until 1949. During his ministry plans were completed for the construction of the Sanctuary, and building was begun, with Brown Whatley as Chairman of the Building Committee.

In 1947, the Larsen Mission was organized into a church, later named Paul Avenue Baptist Church. It serves today as Larsen Outreach Center---still ministering to the same neighborhood for 69 years.

The Sanctuary was occupied for the first time September 10, 1950. The link joining the Sanctuary and the Educational Building was completed October 11, 1953. The new Educational Building was opened October 20, 1957, and for the first time in the church's history all of the activities of the church were housed in church buildings.

San Pablo Mission was established on April, 28, 1954, and Lakewood/San Jose Mission on January 2, 1955. San Pablo Mission was organized into Emmanuel Baptist Church. Lakewood/San Jose Mission became San Jose Baptist Church.

In 1962, Holiday Hill Chapel was established.

In 1963, additional church property was purchased and the church voted to add a visitation evangelist to the staff. Southside's growing concern for missions is evidenced in the fact that for many years she has stood second out of all the churches in Florida in gifts to Missions.

During his time, Dr. Knight served as Moderator of the Jacksonville Baptist Association, President of the Florida Baptist Convention, and President of the Trustees of Midwestern Baptist Seminary.

In 1972, along with Hendricks Avenue Baptist Church, Southside underwrote the construction of the Mt. Olive Baptist Church on Grant Road.

In 1980, Fruit Cove Baptist Church was established.

In 1988, the Trotter Activity Center & McGuire Fellowship Hall were built to better serve the congregation and the San Marco community. Included in this project was the addition of the parking lot behind the north side of the square, providing additional parking in San Marco for the Church and local businesses.

In 2005, helped establish MissionWay Church.

Southside continues to fulfill its mission vision by planting new churches. The Southside Karen Baptist Church, which serves a refugee people group from Burma/Myanmar, was the largest ethnic church plant in Florida Baptist history and meets in the SSBC facility. Southside also played a key role in starting TheCity.Church, a congregation that targets millennials, which currently holds services at Landon Middle School. Our international mission efforts include supporting a team of church planters in France.

Source: Barbara Carroll, Southside Baptist Church.

Southside Karen Baptist Church – 1435 Atlantic Blvd.

Pastor: Thu Lai Mu 2012-Present

Southside's Karen Ministry began when Jacksonville was chosen as a relocation city for refugees from Myanmar, formerly known as Burma. Southside Baptist Church's after-school tutoring and English as a Second Language programs were starting points for many of the Karen, who then began coming to Sunday school and worship services. As the numbers increased, it became apparent that the group needed a worship service and Bible study in their own language, and

Thu Lai Mu joined Southside's staff as pastor to the Karen. In July of 2012, the Southside Karen Baptist Church was constituted and recognized by the convention as the largest ethnic church plant in Florida Baptist history. Over 200 Karen men, women, and children worship and study God's word every week.

Southside United Methodist – 3120 Hendricks Avenue

Ministers:

Bruce Jones	2006 – Present
Wayne D. Wiatt	1996-2006
Dale Tedder	1993-1995, 1999-Present
Jeffrey D. Hoy	1993-1995
Alonzo Davis	1991-1993
Scott K. Echols	1991-1993
Victor B. Willis	1989-1991
Matthew Hartsfield	1987-1989
Charles P. Hamilton	1986-1994
Mac Steimey	1984-1987
John H. Green	1983-1985
C. Dennis McCullough	1980-1983
Ralph B. Huston	1977-1981
Robert G. Bruce, Jr.	1976-1980
Robert C. Boggs	1973-1977
Roger C. Dean	1973-1976
Monroe C. Hatch	1970-1973, 1985-2004
H. Fred Spencer	1970-1973
Frank D. Seibert, Jr.	1966-1970
John S. Bird	1964-1966
Paul Jones	1962-1963
John Sikes	1961-1963
James E. Ridgeway	1959-1961

James E. Compton	1958-1964
Jack Anderson	1956-1961
Frank T. Stoff, Jr.	1955-1957
James C. Rowan	1953-1955
Raymond A. Alley	1950-1956
Bruce Gannaway	1956

1938 – Members of Hendricks Memorial Methodist Church, under the leadership of Reverend Bruce F. Gannaway, envisioned moving from a small land-locked church to a more spacious campus with adequate room to grow.

1949 – After a decade of delay during World War II, a charter was granted to organize Southside Methodist Church.

1950 – The Education Building was completed in time for the first worship Service on Easter Sunday, April 9. There were a total of 550 charter members. Soo, the congregation began to build a sanctuary facing the point of a much traveled road.

1955 – The first worship service in the new sanctuary was celebrated on Palm Sunday, April 3.

1960 –The building connecting the original Education structure with the Langley and the Sanctuary was completed as the congregation observed its 10th Anniversary.

1968 – When Methodist denominations merged with the Evangelical United Brethren, our name officially changed to Southside United Methodist Church.

1995 – The Davis Family Life Center was built as a multipurpose theater for church and community activities while the original Education Building was remodeled to serve as a hub of children's activities and week-day pre-school.

2000 – The congregation celebrated its 50th anniversary with a year-long Jubilee of commemorative events.

2005-2009 – We committed to extensive repairs and refurbishing of the interiors of all building. Along with several other designated projects, we installed a new air conditioning system, rebuilt the Shantz organ, reconfigured and completely refurnished the Chancel area, choir loft, alter rail and youth basement.

2011 – The church replaced the slate roof on all campus buildings.

Source: SSUMC Directory

St. Mark's Evangelical Lutheran Church –
3976 Hendricks Avenue
Pastors:

Robert Hale, interim
December 20, 2015 – present

Thomas S. Hanson
October 1, 2010 — December 13, 2015

Alan W. Peacock, associate
July 6, 2008 — July 11, 2010

Richard D. Dow
August 23, 2006 — September 26, 2010

David Winter, interim
June 1, 2006 — August 20, 2006

Don Reiter, interim
November 22, 2004 — June 1, 2006

Laura M. Wind, associate
July 1, 1998 — April 30, 2002

William F. Scholl
May 15, 1996 — October 31, 2004

James H. Reeb, interim
December 17, 1995 — May 15, 1996

Robert L. Keys, interim
August 1, 1995 — November 14, 1995

Kathryn B. Baines, associate
April 14, 1985 — September 30, 1995

William B. Trexler
August 26, 1979 — July 31, 1995

Harry L. Biemiller
June 3, 1969 — May 6, 1979

George W. Lingle
July 16, 1964 — 1969

Paul K. Nordsiek
May 15, 1951 — December 31, 1963

George F. Hart
January 1939 — January 30, 1951

History -

St. Mark's Evangelical Lutheran Church started with the dream of the Rev. William J. Ducker, Special Missionary of the Board of American Missions, the Rev. D.W.E. Pugh, President of the Florida Synod, and the Rev. C.F.H. Krueger, Chairman of the Missions Committee. The first meeting of the interested persons with these leaders was held at the J.H. Hinck home on July 6, 1938. The second meeting was held at the home of Dr. and Mrs. F.W. Krueger on July 13. Arrangements were made to hold the first service on July 17, 1938 in the Burns-Naugle Funeral Chapel. By November 13, 50 people were ready to organize a new Lutheran church on the southside of Jacksonville.

1939–1951 Pastor George F. Hart

On December 4, 1938, a Constitution was adopted. The congregation took possession of their first property (the South Jacksonville Presbyterian Church building) on February 1, 1939, at the corner of Hendricks Avenue and LaSalle Street. We think this is the present site of the San Marco Public library or at that intersection. Plans for a new building were developed and lots at 3976 Hendricks Avenue were purchased. In 1948, construction began. The new facilities were dedicated on February 13, 1949. At that time, there was a membership of 88 households with 197 people.

1951–1963 Pastor Paul Nordsiek

Due to increasing attendance, two worship services were started in September 1951. An expansion program became imperative, requiring additional property. A master plot plan for adding a Fellowship Hall, Education Building and Nave was developed. The education building program became first priority, and dedication of the new facility was held July 24, 1955. Several years later, it was name "The Nordsiek Wing."

1969–1979 Pastor Harry L. Biemiller

Renovations to provide more adequate educational administrative facilities took place in 1972-1973. During this period, faceted glass windows were added to the Chapel. The Vicar program was initiated in 1975. The decade concluded with a parish commitment of nearly $25,000 for the LCA Strength for Mission Appeal.

1979–1995 Pastor William B. Trexler and Pastor Kathryn B. Baines (1985–1995)

In 1984 over 600 people attended the dedication of the new worship and renovated fellowship space. Assistant Pastor Kathy Baines and Cantor Jim Rindelaub joined the staff in 1985. The 50th anniversary observance in 1988 included a love offering of $50,000 for community ministry through Lutheran Social Services. Vision 21, a strategic plan for the 1990s was completed in 1989. St. Mark's Ark Child Development Center opened in 1990. A major capital funds campaign, "A Gift for God's Children," took place in 1994. At the 1995 Synod Assembly, Pastor William Trexler was elected Bishop of the Florida-Bahamas Synod for a six-year term. Bishop Trexler took office August 1, 1995. Trexler then called Pastor Baines to serve as one of his assistants. On October 1, 1995 she began her new call as Assistant to the

Bishop. Associate in Ministry Carol Schickel was called to serve during the interim.

1996–2004 Pastor William F. Scholl and Pastor Laura M. Wind (1998–2002)

In May 1996, the Rev. Dr. William F. Scholl accepted a call to serve St. Mark's as Senior Pastor. During his tenure, the church facilities were expanded to include a new fellowship hall, music suite, kitchen, and offices for the church staff. In July 1998, the Rev. Laura M. Wind accepted a call as Associate Pastor. In October 2000, Nancy Smith accepted the position of Director of Sacred Arts, Music, and Liturgy. In 2002, Pastor Wind accepted a call to Epiphany Lutheran Church in Winston-Salem, N.C. After consideration of St. Mark's needs, and the growing number of young families and youth, the congregation decided to call a rostered Associate in Ministry (AIM) who would work primarily with children, youth, and families. In 2002, Shelley Wiskirchen was called to the position of Director-Youth and Family Ministries. A highlight of 2003 was the purchase of a house on London Road immediately adjoining the church property for future use as an education/retreat center.

On October 31, 2004, after more than 8 years of faithful service to St. Mark's, and more than 30 years in the ordained ministry, Pastor Scholl retired. In January 2005, Shelley Wiskirchen accepted a call as Admissions Associate at Southern Lutheran Seminary. In November 2005, Nancy Smith and her family moved to Atlanta, Ga. During a time of great change, St. Mark's was blessed to have Pastor Don Reiter serve as interim pastor. Many members of St. Mark's gave of themselves to keep ministries and programs running smoothly.

2006–2010 Pastor Richard D. Dow and Pastor Alan W. Peacock (2008–2010)

In August 2006, the Rev. Richard W. Dow accepted a call to serve as Senior Pastor.

In November 2006, Tony Cruz accepted the position of Director of Music Ministries. In July 2008, Alan W. Peacock was ordained and installed as Associate Pastor at St. Mark's. The Rev. Alan Peacock resigned July 2010. The Rev. Richard Dow resigned September 2010.

2010 – 2015 Pastor Thomas S. Hanson

The Rev. Thomas S. Hanson began serving as interim pastor on October 1, 2010. Hanson had served as an intentional interim pastor in six congregations, five in Minnesota and one in Florida before coming to St. Mark's. On October 2, 2011, the congregation called him as senior pastor. He was installed on November 20, 2011. In August of 2011, we restarted Vacation Bible School with almost 120 children and 65 volunteers. Since then, VBS has become a favorite part of our outreach and education ministries with 70 to 85 children and more than 60 adults participating each year.

We completed a major upgrade of our pipe organ in 2013 with the addition of 22+ digital ranks. Bach Vespers has again become an important part of our continuing music ministry together with our sponsorship of the San Marco Chamber Music Society that performs five times each year in our nave.

Our outreach is expanding beyond mercy ministries into justice ministries with our involvement with ICARE, a local association of Christians, Unitarians, Jews, and Muslims working for justice in our community. We contributed almost $7,000 to the ELCA Malaria Appeal and a large sum to Heiffer Project during Lent 2014. In August 2014, seven of our members went to Haiti on a mission trip. All say it was a very meaningful and important experience for them. We have also made our building more accessible with ramps at the north door of Fellowship Hall and another into Luther Hall. Automatic door-openers were also installed on the entrance to Luther Hall.

The Rev. Thomas S. Hanson resigned late 2015

Source: www.stmarksjax.org

Swaim Memorial Methodist Church – 1620 Naldo Avenue

1886 - 2011 Pastors serving Swaim: 46 plus

One can believe when viewing a large and beautiful church sanctuary and educational facilities such as at Swaim United Methodist Church that it is something that just happened naturally, much as a mushroom springs up overnight. Such is far from being the case, and especially so in the building of Elizabeth Swaim Memorial United Methodist Church.

More than one hundred and twenty-five years ago a small group of Christians living peacefully and quietly in the shadows of the great live oaks and towering pines on the banks of the beautiful St. John's river, decided to organize a church and erect a building in which they could worship in the village of South Jacksonville. Among the members of this group were Governor Harrison and Chloe Merrick Reed;

Wilbur W. and Elizabeth Swaim; John and Mary Landon and daughters Julia and Minerva; M. and Mrs. Charles W. Kinne; Dr. Charles W. Johnson; John Ashworth; Mr. And Mrs. J.H. Durkee; and Rev. William McWaters.

There was no church in the little village at that time. To attend religious services it was necessary to cross the St. Johns River into the then small city of Jacksonville, or travel out the old St. Augustine Road to a little church at Phillips Station. Crossing of the St. John's River was made by a small ferry which operated during daylight hours. Crossing at night was made by rowboat. There were no paved streets in this small village, no electric lights; transportation was by horse and carriage, or on foot - which was the most common method, as few families could afford the luxury of a horse and buggy.

These few families in this village had been worshipping at Trinity Methodist Episcopal Church across the river in Jacksonville (organized in 1870, founding Pastor John S. Swaim - grandfather of W. W. Swaim). They also attended cottage prayer meetings in South Jacksonville under the leadership of a local pastor by the name of William McWaters. In 1886 they felt the need to organize a church in their village. Little did they realize the great effect their decision was going have in the history of this community, or the far-reaching effects of their action upon the lives of the thousands of people who followed them.

Governor Harrison

During that summer of 1886 an application was made to the Presiding Elder of the Methodist Church governing body in the Jacksonville area for a certificate of authority to organize a new church.

191

Rev. William McWaters, local pastor, received the certificate of authority to organize. He called an organizational meeting for the afternoon of September 27, 1886, to be held in the home of Governor Harrison and Chloe Merrick Reed. The Governor's home was located on what is now the southwest corner of Hendricks Avenue and Louisa Street. This was a very nice looking two-story home with porches upstairs and downstairs across the front. There was a white picket fence running around the house to keep out the livestock that roamed the streets in those days. A brick walk ran from the front gate to the house steps. Midway down the walk was an arched trellis covered by a climbing rose bush.

With joy in their hearts, the Board of Trustees appointed by the Presiding Elder stepped down the walk and under the rose arch that warm September afternoon, realizing they were taking the first steps to bring into reality a long cherished dream.

Rev. McWaters called the meeting to order. He stated the objective of the meeting and presented the certificate from the Presiding Elder, which read:

"This is to certify that I have this day appointed the Honorable Harrison Reed, Dr. C. W. Johnson, Charles W. Kinne, W. W. Swaim, and John Ashworth, a Board of Trustees for the Grace Methodist Episcopal Church in Oklahoma or South Jacksonville, said Board to hold office until a Quarterly Conference shall be convened and a Board shall be elected." Signed: J. H. Stoney, Presiding Elder

Grace Methodist Episcopal Church

Rev. William McWaters was appointed the first pastor of Grace Methodist Episcopal Church, Mrs. Harrison (Chloe Merrick) Reed was appointed Sunday School Superintendent, and Mrs. W. W. (Elizabeth) Swaim and Miss Mary Booth were appointed teachers of the Sunday school. And with that - the humble beginnings of our church had taken root!
Finding our home…

Meetings were held in homes for a short period of time. In November of 1886, Grace church secured the use of the Temperance Hall to hold services. The Board selected a church building plan submitted by the Board of Missions and Church Extension. The building size was 32 feet by 50 feet. The members went out to try and raise money, but money was scarce back in those days, and headway was slow. To make matters worse, in the summer of 1887 the yellow fever epidemic broke out. Church services were
temporarily discontinued.

Two years later in early 1889, the church was reorganized. Miss Julia Landon was appointed Financial Secretary. The plans to build the church were again taken up but progress was still slow. The membership was small - between 18 - 20 people - and for the most part made up of people with moderate means. The Sunday worship service collection was less than $2.00. Attendance at Sunday School slightly better, averaging 20 - 25 persons, but an average collection of less than 50 cents.

The next year, 1890, the first Building Committee was appointed: Miss Julia Landon, Mrs. John (Mary) Landon, W. W. Swaim, and Mrs. J. H. Burst. The prospects for the church were discouraging in the 1890s. In a pastor's report, Rev. Presbry stated that the future looked dark. People were reluctant to join the church, fearing that the building would not be finished. He stated he was able to do but little pastoral work, for his time was taken up with laboring on the new building. However, he ended the report by saying he was hopeful for a brighter future of temporal and spiritual prosperity. In 1891 Potter Palmer, Francis Cornish, Mrs. R.D. Root and Pastor A.A. Paisley were added to the Building Committee.

In 1893, the finished building was dedicated by Bishop Foster.

In 1900 the church building was moved from its location of what is now the 1500 block of Montana Street to what is now 1064 Kings Road. The parsonage was erected adjoining the church at what is now 1062 Kings Road. The value of the church was $2,000.00 and of the parsonage $650.00.

In 1919 agitation for a new building began... Efforts were put made to secure a new building fund. Keep in mind, World War I had just ended, and people had been making fairly good money for their labor during the war. A significant amount of pledges were secured and the future was looking bright. But - as conditions began to recede back to normal, many who had pledged moved to other places, while others made pledges without being able to meet them.

So, in 1922 a decision was made to trade the parsonage at 1062 Kings Road for two empty lots. Those lots were at what is now LaSalle Street and Naldo Avenue, where the sanctuary still stands today. By 1923 a Building Committee was appointed with E.H. Vrieze, President of the Board of Trustees, as chairman.

In 1924 M.C. Greeley was engaged as Architect, and building plans were finally adopted that year. In 1925 the contract for construction was let to O.P. Woodcock Company. Ground was broken on March 8. The cornerstone was placed on April 5 by District Superintendent J.J. Treadwell. And finally - on December 13, 1925 the church was opened, dedicated, and renamed the Elizabeth Swaim Memorial Methodist Church.

Elizabeth Caroline Booth Swaim, born August 7, 1867 in Berry, Canada, moved to Jacksonville with her father and sisters when she was a young lady. She attended Snyder Memorial Methodist Church where she met Captain Wilbur Welling Swaim of New Jersey. They were married September 15, 1885. Mrs. Swaim was the first Sunday School teacher and was active in the Ladies Aid Society. Mrs. Swaim passed away February 13, 1924 and Capt. Swaim died December 25, 1938.

Making an imprint…

Elizabeth Swaim Memorial United Methodist Church, or Grace Methodist Episcopal Church as it originally was called, is directly related to the visionary founders of modern Florida. Four of those organizers were Governor Harrison and Chloe M. Reed, and Wilbur and Elizabeth Swaim. The church still shows their visionary hallmarks. It is one of the few churches in Florida dedicated as a memorial to a woman: two-thirds of its stained glass windows honor women - members of the congregation, relatives of members, and women's groups. And, over a century ago, the church had Julia Landon serving as a leader. Elizabeth Swaim Memorial United Methodist Church is not just any church. Since the early decades of the last century, it proclaimed that women are vital parts of both the community and the church. Then, this church translated those beliefs into a physical reality for all to see. E. Swaim Memorial U.M.C. is a building with an extraordinary history a and community symbol - "The Church of the Lighted Cross" - of the human hunger for a close relationship with the living, loving Creator.

Provided by Ryan Buckley

The Church of Jesus Christ of Latter-Day Saints –
4087 Hendricks Avenue

Stake President – Stephen Heywood

In March of 1894, the State of Florida was made part of the Southern States Mission for The Church of Jesus Christ of Latter Day Saints. In 1845, Phineas Young, Brother of Brigham Young gave copies of the Book of Mormon to the Indian Chiefs in Florida. The first missionary work began in the Suwanee County Area. Missionary work began in Jacksonville, Florida in 1897. The first Florida Conference was held in the Jacksonville Park Opera House. The first LDS chapel with a bell tower was at the corner of Claude and Short Streets in Jacksonville.

In 1908, Charles A. Callis, a former Florida Missionary, became the President of the Southern States Mission. Elder Callis had been born in Dublin, Ireland and was a member of the Utah and Florida Bar Associations. He served as President of the Southern States Mission for 27 years. He later became a

196

member of the Quorum of the Twelve Apostles in 1934. On December 10, 1926 David O. McKay, the Church President, dedicated a chapel at Park and Copeland. Charles Callis was later referred to as the "Shepard of the South."

In 1955 the ground breaking for the Florida Stake Tabernacle (4087 Hendricks Avenue) took place. Its value was $400,000 but was built for $248, 000 due to the sweat equity donated by the members of the church. More than 14,000 man-hours were donated during its construction.

Due to the huge growth in membership in 1968, the Florida Stake with approximately 5,825 members and 11 wards (local congregations) was divided. (The term *Stake* is an intermediate level in the organizational hierarchy of The Church of Jesus Christ of Latter-Day Saints.) Jacksonville Stake became the Jacksonville Florida East Stake and the Jacksonville Florida West Stake. L. Blaine Vorwaller became the Jacksonville Florida West Stake President. Harold B. Lee, President of the Church, left Salt Lake City to preside at the 25th anniversary of the Stake in 1972. In 1997, President Gordon B. Hinckley attended the 50th Anniversary celebration.

In 1978 L. Blaine Vorwaller was set apart as a Regional Representative by Elder LeGrand Richards. In 1997 the Jacksonville North Stake was created and in 1989 the total Church members in Florida was 82,000. President Gordon B. Hinckley officiated at the 50th Anniversary of the Southern Stake. By 1993 the Church membership in Florida grew to over 93,000. In 1994, The Orlando Temple was dedicated by President Howard B. Hunter. Last year the Fort Lauderdale Florida Temple was dedicated. As of 2015, church membership grew to 152,217 in Florida.

President Gordon B. Hinckley said, "The strength of the Church is not in the buildings of the church, it is not in the temples, it is not on the Brigham Young University Campus. The strength of The Church of Jesus Christ of Latter-Day Saints is in the hearts of the people." Today approximately 5,000 members worship in the Jacksonville area.

Information obtained from the text: Salt of the South, The LDS Trail Blazers by La Viece Moore – Fraser Smallwood.

Provided by JoAnne Bridegan

198

Schools

Assumption Catholic School
2431 Atlantic Boulevard

The original Assumption School was constructed at the corner of Gary and Naldo Streets in 1923.

In 1948 land was purchased on Atlantic Boulevard. The existing building on the property, which was formerly the Merrill-Stevens Shipyard Administration Building, was converted into a school. This new Assumption School opened in September 1949 with 317 students.

In 1954 six additional classrooms are added.

In 1965 the fifth through eighth grade classrooms were built along with the Parish Hall. These additional buildings allowed the school to convert the old auditorium into a library and media center.

In 1977 a new Activity Center was built freeing the Parish Hall for school use. A preschool for three and four year olds was implemented and in 1996 the original school building was completely renovated and updated.

The Assumption faculty and administration has also changed dramatically since the school started. In the early years of Assumption from 1923-1969, the principal and teachers were primarily nuns. Sister Patricia Eileen Consier was the last principal who was a nun. Since 1977 the principal has been a lay Catholic. Today the teaching staff and principal are all lay Catholics.

Mrs. Maryann Jimenez is the current principal of Assumption Catholic School.

Assumption is one of the oldest parochial schools in Jacksonville. The Assumption community looks forward to the future knowing that the school has been built on a solid foundation with principles and values that remain unchanged in an ever increasing, changing society.

Source: www.assumptionjax.org

Bishop Kenny High School
1055 Kingman Avenue

Bishop Kenny High School is a private, college preparatory, co-educational Catholic high school located on a 55 acre campus . The founder, Archbishop Joseph Patrick Hurley, established the school in 1952, following the merger of three previous Catholic high schools in the Jacksonville area. Bishop Kenny High School was renamed in honor of Bishop William John Kenny, the third bishop of the Diocese of St. Augustine. Bishop Kenny's sports teams are commonly known by their "Crusaders" nickname. In their 60-year history, the school's varsity sports teams have won thirty-seven state team championships.

In recent years the school has expanded substantially. In 2011 The Carla Harris Performing Arts Center was opened. The center seats 450 and features a three-and-a-half story stage facility with dressing rooms, prop and material storage rooms and sound and lighting systems.

In 2014 a $1.6 million building and renovation project was completed improving academic and technology programs, the arts, and stadium facilities. The Demetree Learning Commons, located on the site of the original school library is a redesigned learning and technology headquarters for students. It provides PC workstations for students, in addition to the iPad which each student has.

A permanent art gallery for student art has been established for students interested in the arts.

William Johnston Stadium, home to the Bishop Kenny Crusaders, also underwent a substantial makeover with a new larger press box able to facilitate live radio broadcasts as well as a new concession facility.

Source: www.bishopkenny.org

Hendricks Avenue Elementary
3400 Hendricks Avenue
National Model School. Founded in 1942.

Principals

2012-Pres.	Lacy Healy
2010-2012	Robert "BR" Rhoads
2003-2010	Jayne Owens-Thompson
1994-2003	Emmy Peters
1993-1994	Betty McNamara
1963-1993	Juanita Wilson
1958-1962	Ennis Woodley
19??-1958	Lorena Johnson

Teachers of the Year

2016 – Christina MacDowell
2015 – Mandi York
2014 – Lauren Olesiak
2013 – Cheryl Pearthree
2012 – Rose Hanson
2011 – Kristina Knox
2010 – Tracy Langley
2009 – Melissa Buchanan
2008 – Christa Ritchie
2007 – Beth Seeker
2006 – Kristen Whitaker

**Julia Landon College Prep/
Landon Jr. & Sr. High**
1819 Thacker Avenue.
Built in 1927

Principals

2015-Pres.	Timothy M. Feagins
2012-2013	Sara Bravo
2008-2012	Dr. Kelly Coker-Daniel
2006-2008	Mark Ertel
2003-2006	Jacquelyn Christopher
1999-2003	Carole Benson
1997-1999	Jane Condon
1993-1997	Elaine Mann
1990-1993	William M. Dutter
1983-1990	Jerry M. Jackson
1976-1979	Roy Grete
1974-1976	John E. Thombleson

1969-1974	John T. Rowell
1965-1969	Robert "Pop" Warner
1945-1965	George H. Wood
1940-1945	James L. McCord
1928-1940	William H. Turney
1927-1928	RC Marshall

Teachers of the Year

2016-2017 – Tamela Lively
2015-2016 – Kristopher Beckstrom
2014-2015 – Stacey Johnson
2013-2014 – Sharlie Conklin
2012-2013 – Kristie Putnal
2011-2012 – Donna Long
2010-2011 – Jean Spiwak
2009-2010 – Robyn Wilhelm

South Jacksonville Grammar School
1450 Flagler Avenue
Built in 1916

SJGS was designed by Mark and Sheftall architects, students of Henry J Klutho. It was built in 1916 and was a public elementary school until 1971 and then became a supply depot for Duval County Public Schools. In 2001 it was sold and was converted to private residences and office space by the Cesery Company and is now known as The Lofts San Marco. In 2004 the building was placed on the National Register of Historic Places.

Other schools that serve San Marco residents:

The Bolles School

Douglas Anderson School of the Arts

Darnell Cookman Middle School

Dupont Middle School

Episcopal Middle School and High School

James Weldon Johnson Middle School

Kirby Smith Middle School

LaVilla School of the Arts

Paxon College Preparatory School

Stanton College Preparatory School

Wolfson High School

Government Leaders

Mayors

Lenny Curry	2015-Incumbant
Alvin Brown	2011-15
John Peyton	2003-2011
John Delaney	1995-2003
Ed Austin, Jr.	1991-1995
Tommy Hazouri	1987-1991
Jake Godbold	1979-1987
Hans Tanzler	1967-1979
Lou Ritter	1965-1967
W. Haydon Burns	1949-1965
Frank Whitehead	1945-1949
John T. Alsop, Jr.	1941-1945
George C. Blume	1937-1941
John T. Alsop, Jr.	1923-1937

City Council Members

Lori Boyer	2011-Incumbant
Art Shad	2003-2011
Matt Carlucci	1999-2003
George Banks	1995-1999
Howard Dale	1994-1995
Ginny Myrick	1987-1994
Gifford Grange	1979-1987
John F. Lanahan, Sr.	1967-1979
William Henry Miles	1933-1950

Clubs and Organizations

Boy Scouts of America - Troop 35

Scoutmasters

Adam McDonough
Chris Knowling
Reese Comer
Jan White
Paige Preston (father of David Preston Swaim)

Eagle Scouts

Dylan Tedder	July 27, 2016
Ryan Lee Garner	December 7, 2015
Matthew J. Knowling	October 26, 2015
Austin Saltmarsh	October 12, 2015
Jesse M. Evans	March 12, 2015
Bradford J. Bailey	October 25, 2014
Hunter Bailey Wilson	May 29, 2014
Hamilton T. Eng	May 19, 2014
Andrew Callahan	August 8, 2013
Philip P. Kenny	June 24, 2013
James W. Cooksey	December 7, 2011
Ian A. Murphy	October 3, 2011
Daniel Z. Fischer	April 11, 2011
Andrew James Price	May 17, 2010
John David Searcy	April 22, 2010
Daniel Ryan King	January 16, 2010
Robert S. Highsmith	August 17, 2009
Lane G. Wright	July 23, 2007
Travis E. Comer	June 14, 2007

Joshua Lewis Green	January 29, 2007
Charles D. LaPrade	January 22, 2007
Jennings B. Cooksey IV	October 29, 2006
Jared Patten Mathis	September 25, 2006
Joshua B. Cooksey	August 14, 2006
Bradley Sheffield	October 10, 2005
Stewart Michael Collins	April 25, 2005
Morgan Patrick Andrews	April 10, 2005
Brian Joseph Hofrichter	April 4, 2005
Ronald J. Nemeyer	September 26, 2004
Weston G. Andrews	September 12, 2004
Holland Harris, Jr.	December 4, 2003
Joseph G. Foote	October 30, 2003
Seth Mollitt	September 18, 2003
Reece Comer III	June 5, 2003
Paul Black	June 2003
Tommy King	May 15, 2003
Alan Williams	April 18, 2003
Austin Morales	
Daniel Morris	May 2002
Frank Leli	February 19, 2001
Daniel Bidleman	March 22, 1999
Neal Turbow	July 8, 1999
Matthew Wiatt	December 12, 1998
Chad Forester	October 26, 1998
Alan Melvin	January 29, 1998
Todd Mollitt	November 15, 1996
Joseph Summerfild	April 11, 1990
Jason Winters	August 21, 1989
John Desalvo	March 7, 1988
Carl Philips	October 1986
Danny Barrow	May 1986
David Stoddard	April 1985
David Preston	June 1980

John Yost	September 1976
William LaPrade	June 17, 1974
Mike Shenerd	January 1971
Charles Lever	September 29, 1970
Gene Blackwell	June 2, 1970
Mark Preston	December 1969
Robert M. Dickenson, II	April 1969
Clifford Herrington	October 1968
Chauncey W. Lever Jr.	February 1967
Donnie Beck	January 11, 1960
Bobby Schondelmaier	August 10, 1959
David Seitz	August 10, 1959
Frank Brennan	August 10, 1959
Merrill Shore	August 10, 1959
David Davenburg	August 10, 1959
Steve Leach	August 10, 1959
Tommy Leach	August 10, 1959
Leslie Seitz	February 9, 1959
Tommy Lee	December 9, 1957
Andy Hogan	June 1957
Tommy Register	January 14, 1952
Dick Fulton	November 25, 1941
Raymond Beck	December 1940
Henry Berline	February 23, 1939
James Parks	February 23, 1939
Arthur Goodhue	January 26, 1939
George Humphries	September 23, 1938
Eugene Schramel	September 23, 1938
Jack Choate	1933

Boy Scouts of America Troop 106

Eagle Scouts

Nino Mah	2016
Matthew Considine	2016
Will Haubner	2016
Andrew Considine	2015
Jonathan Barnes	2015
Nick Herro	2015
Charlie Wilkinson	2015
Philip Thomas	2014
Nicholas Chitty	2014
Jeremy Barnes	2014
Geoffrey Heekin	2013
Austin McGowan	2013
Sam Heekin	2013
Adam Ephrem	2012
Davis Shaw	2012
Michael Herro	2012
Franco Bautista	2011
Michael Holmes	2011
Alex Sikorski	2011
Reno Varghese	2010
George Soha	2009
David Soha	2009
Joe Soha	2009
Brent Laurint	2009
Chris Dean	2009
Charles Herro	2008
Zack Dumstorf	2008
Chris Snowden	2008

David Perera	2006
Joe Herro	2006
Paulo Bautista	2006
Kyle Curran	2006
Michael Hartley	2006
Bill Bishop	2006
Chris Soha	2006
Thomas Heekin	2006
Michael Davlantes	2006
Ed Duffy	2005
Kevin Heekin	2005
Tim Lanahan	2005
Ray Soha	2004
Steven Kelly	2004
Chad Snowden	2003
Mike Soha	2002
Chris Lazo	2002
Eric Serrano	2001
John Weedon	1999
Ray Heekin	1999
Matthew Lanahan	1999
Matt Laufenberg	1998
Sheldon Ying	1998
Brendan Bledsoe	1998
John Heekin	1998
Bryan Holtz	1995
Chris Bertozzi	1995
Jamey Weedon	1994
Greg McClellan	1993
Brandon Bascelli	1993
Daniel Serrano	1993
David Heekin	1992
Phil Cohn	1991
Randy White, Jr.	1989

Rob Heekin, Jr.	1987
Koorosh Reyhani	1985
Cliff Simpson	1985
Victor Newsome	1983
Chris Swan	1980
Mark Heekin	1977
John Bunker	1977
Patrick Heekin	1975
Geoff Heekin	1972
Mark Swan	1971
Mike Bunker	1970
Patrick McKee	1968
David Heekin	1968
Mike Heekin	1967
Rob Heekin	1965
Chuck Lightner	1965
Jim Heekin, Jr.	1964
Charles Heekin	1964
Mike Lightner	1964
Jim Caliri	1964
Michael Lanahan	1956
Michael Golay	1956
Jack Duval	1956
Roger Williams	1955
Dennis Lanahan	1955
Bob McCallum	1955
Daniel Chichester	1953
Charles Breen	1953
Billy Christian	1952

Boy Scouts of America Troop 136

<u>Scoutmasters</u>

Scott Le Hockey	2011 – Present
Scott Norton	2011 – 2016
Gene Hurst Jr.	2005 – 2011
Al Poindexter	2000 – 2005

<u>Eagle Scouts</u>

Ben Swanson	2016
Jarrett Elson	2016
Daniel Norton	2016
Drew Portell	2015
Matthew Cunningham	2014
Alec Byers	2014
Ross Johnson	2014
Alex J. Bongers	2013
Ryan A. Bjork	2012
Andrew L. Hurst	2011
William T. Shubrick	2011
Collin F. Lingaitis	2010
Jerry Edwards	2009
Thomas L. Hurst	2009
William W. Law	2008
Thomas S. Edwards, IV	2008
David J. Cortez	2007
Joseph B. Dougherty	2007
Colin J. Doak	2007
Gene A. Hurst, Jr.	2006
Brian M. Childers	2006
James C. Poindexter	2005

Girls Scouts

Editor's note: We were unable to separate out the Girl Scout awards by zip code, so we have included all Gateway Council recipients in this list.

The top award in Girl Scouts has changed through the years... Here is your quick guide.

1982- Current:	Gold Award.
1963-1982:	First Class
1940-1963:	Curved Bar
1938-1940:	First Class
1919-1938:	Golden Eaglet
1912-1919:	Golden Eagle of Merit

Gold Awards

2015 - Jennifer DiLoreto, Allie Fliess, Olivia Jacobi, Emily Lassley, Marisa McCarty, Briana Parker, Breanna Rushlow, Stephanie Thompson.

2014 - Katherina Albers, Jennifer Banks, Steffanie Cassey, Sarah Evans, Julia Faherty, Regan Foote, Katherine Hager, Rachael Howell, Kathleen Johnston, Anna Kelly.

2013 - Caroline Kapcio, Laura Wardrop, Jessica Wells, Leah Wright, Tatum Shannon, Charly Coogan, Sabrina Rule, Bethnie Olivier, Delaney Sagul, Piper McInall, Hope Stevens, Erin Honeycutt, Morgan Green, Breanna Kuchta, Emily Parker, Danielle Cogdell.

2012 - Louise Burton, Christina Grodell, Aliya Jenkins, Dana Ratcliffe, Joslyn Simmons, Jessica Wells.

2011 - Katherine Andux, Maureen Brennan, Ana Bautista, Britney Ezell, Alexandria Fields, Zoee Frazier, Allison Fyffe, Antoinette Danielle Hagins, Alana Hall, Katelin Hobgood.

2010 - Enshera Badu-Tweneboah, Taylor Bennick, Evelyn Abagayle Boyd, Shannon Jean Bradley, Sierra Cunningham, Maria DeCerce, Falon Dominguez, Rachel Fox, Lisa Glenn, Jennifer Gouge, Lindsey Heibert, Leoniqua Jackson, Linda Jenkins, Rebecca Kirby, Kayla Lewis, Carolyn Mercer, Samantha Mink, Jackie Nettles, Autum Shaw, Lauren Slavens, Paige Smola, Emily Tate, Isabel Teller, Lawren Turner, Hailey Warber, Tiffany Zednek.

2009 - Christiana Broughton, Aria Clark, Danyelle Eldridge, Angela Epifano, Alexis Gallo, Jessica Gearhard, Rudie Gillett, Sarah Hughes, Lauren Isabelle, Annette Jubert, Caitlyn Kendrick, Michelle Lyman, Heather Mutchie, Song Naber, Emily Pendergraft, Bonita Phillips, Christine Rosatone, Chelsea Stanch, Kelsey Walsh.

2008 - Jordan Benton, Jessica Brown, Julia Butler, Katelyn Carter, Jennifer Ciuffetelli, Jordan DECoy, Megan Gillespie, Hannah Jones, Kelcie Lloyd, Hope Margaret Olexa, Sarah Pendergraft, Melinda Picciuolo, Jennifer Reid, Amanda Solomons, Carlina Williams, Jacqueline Wood.

2007 - Jessie Blalock, Alexandra Connor, Ashlee Cooper, Rachel Crisler, Julia Fallon, Samantha Goulet, Kelsey Henderson, Dione Johnson, Corissa Larkins, Jenna Johnson, Breana Link, Margaret Luther, Loren McLendon, Lynn Papapetrou, Rhiannon Roach, Sarah Shoffner, Danielle Sanders, Nisha Tahiliani, Hillary Weaver, Carol Bunker, Kelly Watson.

2006 - Stephanie Babcock, Catherine Barnes, Amanda Basara, Sarah Beckett, Jeanine Blake, Sarah Brezil, Elaina Buono, Amanda Ciuffetelli, Juliet Diaz, Brigitte Donovan-High, Krystal Dreyer, Talia Fleet, Katie Foster, Kimberly Hall, Krystina Harcourt, Alycia Hughes, Melissa Leonard, Brittany Martin, Amanda Maroney, Leigh Morris, Amy Neu, Kayla Obergfoll, Juliet Ochs, Kelly Olson,

Andrea Ramirez, Ashley Richardson, Selena Sanderson, Magan Smith, Allison Van Sickle, Stacey Walston, Ashley Webb, Catherine Woodcock.

2005 - Courtney Anderson, Jasmine Anderson, Megan Anderson, Ashley Baldwin, Amelia Benson, Jessica Brantley, Christine Cavallo, Rachel Crabtree, Crystal Davis, Leslie Dugger, Kelley Erickson, Ashley Flecher, Joy Fox, Katherine Frazier, Katie Hamlin, Andrea Herbin, Rachel Hughes, Ann Hunter, Stephanie Hutchins, Stephanie Kelley, Christina King, Jazmine McCoy, Michelle Morris, Katherine O'Brien, Britanny Rudolph, Lauren Sain, Ashley Shoopman, Aldonia Spratling, Erin Thompson, Danielle Von Stein, Katie Watson, Kimberly Wenger, Allison Williams, Maribeth Wood, Sarah Yost.

2004 - Tracy Bennett, Stephanie Blanc, Kristin Catlin, Reva Cowart, Marcetta Davis, Amanda Foster, Mary Hamm, Heather Heffner, Mary Hutson, Kimberly Kreitzman, Amanda Lewis, Callie Maskell, Mary McIntyre, Sara Minton, Laura Pace, Katherine Perri, Kristen Rudolf, Kathleen Veres, Lauren Yackel.

2003 - Jenna Clevinger, Kristen Farmer, Jenna Grizzell, Whitney Hayes, Stephanie Kauffman, Kristin Keet, Jennifer Maskasky, Lari Edward, Molly McKee, Cristina Resczenski, Christy Saunders, Tiffany Scranton, Elizabeth Spitznagel.

2002 - Linda Butler, Janessa Brooks, Anna Deason, Cherita Givens, Kimberly Kronz, Sarah Richardson, Julie Rachel Riddle, Kelly Wagner.

2001 - Robyn Andres, Vicky Baker, Katie Burns, Courtney Caplin, Nicole Gautreaux, Michele Ing, Kate Johnson, Kaitlin Kovacs, Kaytora Long, Maris Edwards, Christan Mullee, Catherine Neilson, Alana Parks, Annette Rhan, April Searcy, Susanna Sellers, Rebecca Sorenson, Antina Stafford, Tracy Thompson.

2000 - Loni Bonnell, Katherine Condon, Keri Eggleston, Jessica Fleischman, Jennifer Geddes, Amber Hickman, Meghan Hotchkiss, Leah Kamleiter, Marlene Lasa, Kimberly Masuda, Melissa Neu, Jennifer Ricks, Lynette Simmonds, Kathleen Sutherland, Nicole Tappan, Valerie Taylor, Melissa Tison, Coral Williams, Stephanie Woster-Martin.

1999 - Laisay Bond, Caroline Brecht, Eileen Brumitt, Leslie Edenger, Sandra Erickson, Krysta Gayle, Deanna Heaton, Laura Hein, Samantha Hickey, Rachel Hutson, Marah Kvaltine, Kimberly Loliva, Adrian McClain, Erin O'Kon, Morgan Phares, Kelly Pigg, Caroline Richardson, Betsy Smith, Angel Szala, Heather Szala, Laurin Thomas, Jennifer Throop, Meagan Tombaugh, Kimberly Weaver, Heather Wells, Linnea Wingo.

1998 - Aime Carle, Melissa Cheatham, Nicole Downer, Nadirah Edwards, Elizabeth Feeser, Lauren Gossinger, Lee-Anne Julian, Alyssa Krop, Mala Kay Lawrence, Amy MacGillivary, Amber McEldowney, Janice Miklitsch, Sarah Portier, Kiki Puntervold, Karhleen Reemelin, Katie Ridgway, Amanda Sain, Kathleen Simmons, Amie Steward, Teressa Stone, Rebecca Summers, Kimberly Wallis, Sabrina Wright.

1997 - Antoinette Davis, Kristine Erickson, Kyla McGee, Laurel Mosura, Melissa Owens, Alice Rollins, Deborah Thomas, Maggie Willims, Jennifer Andreu, Tiffany Donn, Sara Duncan, Shannon Elholm, Annette Hartley, Jennifer O'Brien, Kathy Ogden, Laura Roberts, Patricia Ross, Erin Scott, Stephanie Smith, Elisa Wern, Ann Buffalo.

1996 - Elizabeth Gibson, Colleen Beaupre, Erica Brooks, Elizabeth Dawn Burkey, Tammy Caplin, Jaclyn Croft, Ayana Grady, Maria Hickman, Angela Schweer, Heather Scott, Jennifer Sivinski, Heather Strickland, Christina Wood.

1995 - Stephanie Ash, Desiree Cauchon, Catherine Detweiler, Shannon Faherty, Florence Folmer, Amy Gibson, Debra Hunt, Julie

Johnson, Alicia Kelley, Susan Kite,Courtney Lloyd, Lindsay Maiman, Tara Mitchell, Anna Mulkey, Lynsey Nellis, Amy Oberholtzer, Kelly Pitts, Tracy Reed, Nicole Reid, Catherine Reynolds, Andrea Ulery, Lindsay Walkup, Erica Weber.

1994 - Heather Burney, Samantha Batten, Jennifer Branch, Jacqueline Brooks, Heather Burney, Rebecca Eick, Mariah Elmore, Kristie Grebe, Mary Howell, Jeannie Irvin, Elaine Jackson, Selena O'Neal, Amanda Parrish, Debra Richards, Katrina Roberts, Rachel Smith-Vaniz, Katherine Thomas, Veronica Vucho, Alfreda Wei.

1993 - Ingrid Rollins, Summer Floyd, Wendy Ferguson, Jennifer Bethune, Latasha Cooper, Dawn Dubay, Jennifer Foltz, Mary Gilman, Carla Grove, Rosalind Johnson, Beth Krzeminski, Dawn Morgan, Sara Plummer, Aveanna Porter, Bobbie Wescott.

1992 - Jeannie Syler, Julie Platt, Suzanne Boles, Miranda Brady, Amy Gardner, Sherri Green,Virginia Groble, Lathrop Hart, Jenny Meredith, Charlotte Olsen, Tiffany Osteen, Jennifer Word.

1991 - Mary Ann Bolin, Dana Bujold, Heather Burrell, Dina Dmytrenko, Polly Eick,Leticia Fields, Deborah Fessler, Melba Furlow, Heather Janssen, Tamara Wilson, Danielle Smith.

1990 - Anne Bouchelle, Jennifer Crawford, Karen Deck, Jeanette Farah, Cari Gibbs Kelly Godfrey, Elizabeth Heath, Lisa Manion, Teresa Olsen, Danielle Smith.

1989 - Cincy Brannen, Sherri Bethune, Shannon Clark, Karen Furillo, Leticia Garcia, Melissa Miller, Melissa Newell, Harriett Rhea, Nadine Greene, Theresa Ricks.

1988 - Sarah Cousins, Tony Friend, Tracy Quarles, Cyprianna Smith, Cincy Brannen, Sherri Bethune, Shannon Clark, Karen Furillo, Leticia Garcia, Melissa Miller, Melissa Newell, Harriett Rhea, Nadine Greene, Theresa Ricks.

1984 - Virginia Barker, Elizabeth Caesar.

1983 - Gwen Whittington, Lisa Miller, Debbie Mann, Nora Allstedt, Vickie Chadwick, Pamela Winstead, Karla Kepner.

1982 - Melanie Helling, Debbie Grimm, Laura Winstead, Jennifer Hudson, Kathy Kerslake, Tracy McAvoy, Sherie Charlton.

1981 - Nancy Blastic, Julie Wise.

First Class

1980 - Judy Dukes, Patty Mullins, Andrea Eaves, Irene Wainwright, Catherine Schoening, Joyce Wainwright, Betsy Yawn, Cheryl Furrow, Rosaland Lennon, Dianne Wood, Melanie Wood, Lynne Johns, Michelle Kimutis, Carmen Eaves, Theresa Ricks.

1979 - Yvette Sturkes, Yvonne Sturkes, Susan Caton, Pam Walker.

1975 - Dee Stallings, Diane Holton.

1973 - Gail Anderson, Yvonne Hall.

1970 - Kathy Bryant, Mickey Cooke, Nancy Edmunds.

1969 - Susan Roberts, Claudia Ruff, Judy Simons, Brenda Thomson, Charlotte Telken, Shelly McKinley, Denise Turner.

1968 - Cynthia McMurray, Janet Fowler, Cheryl Vogel.

Curved Bar

1959 - Nancy Graessle, Harriett L'Engle, Linda Duncan, Jane Jabbour.

1958 - Karen Scanland, Carol Ann Meister, Patsy Garden, Susan Benjamin, Carol Cheney, Mary Beth Davis, Joann Griffin McDurham, Nancy Marks.

1957 - Patsy Marable, Betty Veal, Lois Ellen Graessle, Lynda Pierce, Kay McCormick, Mabelle Clark.

1956 - Barbara Duncan, Evangeline Futch, Peggy Croom, Patricia Avinger, Leila Crawford, Elizabeth Crawford, Elizabeth Tiernan.

1955 - Corrine Germain, Mary Frances King, Peggy Shannon, Mary Alice Barrett.

1954 - Elizabeth Fross, Sandy Roberts, Kay Wood, Bonnie Speth, Judy Anderson, Joan Enge, Marsha Robison.

1952 - Merline Johnson, May Vason, Tamsy Fain, Daisy Kirk.

1950 - Martha Rosser.

1947 - Betty Gena Blanton, Ruth Smith.

1946 - Shirley Roberts.

Golden Eaglet

1931 - Mary Gardener.

1930 - Marie Richards, Virginia Ridgely.

1928 - Harriet Baker.

Source: Patricia Knowles, Girl Scouts of Gateway Council.

San Marco Garden Circle

Editor's note: Further information about the San Marco Garden Circle can be found in Jan Bebeau, Georgia Dahl, and Suzanne Perritt's essay on page 36 and Cathy Watkiss's on page 145.

<u>Presidents</u>

2015-2016	Co-Pres., Lindsey Riggs & Shari Thanner
2014-2015	Paula Joyner
2013-2014	Paula Joyner
2012-2013	Co-Pres., Sherrill Mullens & Wendy LaPrade
2011-2012	Co-Pres., Sherrill Mullens & Wendy LaPrade
2010-2011	Jan Bebeau
2009-2010	Jan Bebeau
2008-2009	Susan Cheney
2007-2008	Susan Cheney
2006-2007	Suzanne Perritt
2005-2006	Suzanne Perritt
2004-2005	Noel Liles
2003-2004	Noel Liles
2002-2003	Wendy LaPrade
2001-2002	Wendy LaPrade
2000-2001	Bonnie Henry
1999-2000	Bonnie Henry
1998-1999	Mary Green
1997-1998	Mary Green
1996-1997	Mary Green
1995-1996	Mrs. Dale E. Watkiss
1994-1995	Mrs. James H. Dahl
1993-1994	Mrs. Brown Barnes
1992-1993	Mrs. Brown Barnes
1991-1992	Mrs. Harry Graves
1990-1991	Mrs. Denmark Puckett
1989-1990	Mrs. Denmark Puckett

1988-1989	Mrs. Robert M. Barnes
1987-1988	Mrs. Frank T. Scott
1986-1987	Mrs. Lee Bransford, Jr.
1985-1986	Mrs. J. Lamar Smith
1984-1985	Mrs. George Wood
1983-1984	Mrs. Hubert L. Ponder
1982-1983	Mrs. Hubert L. Ponder
1981-1982	Mrs. Jose Zubero
1980-1981	Mrs. George Wood
1979-1980	Mrs. John Q. U. Thompson
1978-1979	Mrs. Lee E. Bransford, Jr.
1977-1978	Mrs. Hubert L. Ponder
1976-1977	Mrs. Hubert L. Ponder
1975-1976	Mrs. J. Lamar Smith
1974-1975	Mrs. Frank T. Scott
1973-1974	Mrs. Frank T. Scott
1972-1973	Mrs. Theodore W. Glocker, Jr.
1971-1972	Mrs. Theodore W. Glocker, Jr.
1970-1971	Mrs. Clinton Burbridge
1969-1970	Mrs. Clinton Burbridge
1968-1969:	Mrs. Donald E. Bishop
1967-1968	Mrs. Donald E. Bishop
1966-1967	Mrs. Robert A. Harris
1965-1966	Mrs. Ivan J. Mitchell
1964-1965	Mrs. Ivan J. Mitchell
1963-1964	Mrs. William C. McDonough
1962-1963	Mrs. William C. McDonough
1961-1962	Mrs. J. Lamar Smith
1960-1961	Mrs. J. Lamar Smith
1959-1960	Mrs. Eugene A. Griffith
1958-1959	Mrs. Hal W. Moore
1957-1958	
1956-1957	Mrs. Edward P. Mulcahy
1955-1956	Mrs. Edward P. Mulcahy

1954-1955	Mrs. Eugene Griffith
1953-1954	Mrs. Charles J. Regero
1952-1953	Mrs. Charles J. Regero
1951-1952	Mrs. James French, Jr.
1950-1951	Mrs. James French, Jr.
1949-1950	Mrs. J. E. Graves, Jr.
1948-1949	Mrs. George P. Norris
1947-1948	Mrs. George P. Norris
1946-1947	Mrs. Richard E. Gerrish
1945-1946	Mrs. Richard E. Gerrish
1944-1945	Mrs. H. Austin Bliss
1943-1944	Mrs. Oscar Blasingame
1942-1943	Mrs. Oscar Blasingame
1941-1942	Mrs. E. H. Vrieze, Jr.
1940-1941	Mrs. Robert A. Harris
1939-1940	Mrs. Robert A. Harris
1938-1939	Mrs. Karl Bardin
1937-1938	
1936-1937	Mrs. C. A. Kimbel
1935-1936	
1934-1935	Mrs. Brown Whatley
1933-1934	Mrs. Albert A. Lawton
1932-1933	Mrs. A. J. Ives

San Marco Merchants Association

The San Marco Merchants Association (SMMA), a not-for-profit organization, seeking to unify the business groups in the area with a collective voice to help promote the area as destination to locals and visitors alike.

Presidents

2016 – Anita Vining
2015 – Anita Vining
2014 – Kiley Efron
2013 – George Foote
2012 – George Foote
2011 – Desiree Bailey
2010 – Tim Shurling/Desiree Bailey
2009 – Jane Bracken
2008 – Janet Molyneaux
2007 – Janet Molyneaux
2006 – Ryan Buckley
2005 – Karl "Jay" Jabour
2004 – Jennifer Price
1990 – Janet Hoven

San Marco Preservation Society

The San Marco Preservation Society was formed in 1975 as a non-profit corporation to protect the integrity of the San Marco residential neighborhood and to enhance the revitalization of the business district. Many active members have succeeded in keeping the old-world charm and character of San Marco intact.

South Jacksonville City Hall located at 1468 Hendricks Avenue was designed by the noted Jacksonville architectural firm of Mark and Sheftall. It was constructed in 1915 and is one of the few remaining visual reminders of the City of South Jacksonville. It was designated a local landmark in 2002. In July, 2003 SMPS took over the building and took on the task of

224

renovation and restoration of the building. On January 21, 2008, San Marco Preservation held a grand opening of the newly restored building which now serves as its headquarters. SMPS received an award for this project from the Florida Trust for Historic Preservation in 2009.

San Marco Preservation Hall is also maintained by SMPS and is a Jacksonville historic landmark. It was built in 1888 as St. Paul's Episcopal Church. In 1994, this beautiful and charming building was moved to Fletcher Park at 1652 Atlantic Boulevard and renovated. It is frequently used as a rental facility for weddings, parties, and meetings.

Presidents

2016 – 2017   LeAnna Cumber
2015 – 2016   Andrew Dickson
2014 – 2015   Mary Toomey
2013 – 2014   Reese Riggle
2012 – 2013   Diane Martin
2011 – 2012   Doug Skiles
2010 – 2011   Jon Singleton
2009 – 2010   George Foote
2008 – 2009   Valerie Feinberg Evans
2007 – 2008   Richard Moore, Jr.
2006 – 2007   Rob Smith
2005 – 2006   Tim Martin
2004 – 2005   Lori Boyer
2003 – 2004   Lori Boyer
2002 – 2003   Mark McLean
2001 – 2002   Jennifer Newman
2000 – 2001   Robin Robinson
1999 – 2000   Roger Clarke

1998 – 1999	Pat Andrews
1997 – 1998	Paul Saffell
1996 – 1997	Yvonne Corey
1995 – 1996	Chris Hixenbaugh
1994 – 1995	Lori Nemeyer Boyer
1993 – 1994	Rob Smith
1992 – 1993	Suzanne Perritt
1991 – 1992	Brian McCabe
1991 – 1992	Grier Wells
1990 – 1991	Yvonne Corey
1989 – 1990	Terry Moore
1988 – 1989	Wade Hampton
1987 – 1988	Skip Allcorn
1986 – 1987	Skip Allcorn
1985 – 1986	Connie Gesvaldi, Judy Blumberg
1984 – 1985	Tom Reynolds, Connie Gesvaldi
1983 – 1984	Tom Reynolds
1982 – 1983	Tom Reynolds, Cathryn Lee
1981 – 1982	Steve Tool
1980 – 1981	Jim Rink
1979 – 1980	Jim Rink
1978 – 1979	Lee Mercier
1977 – 1978	Jay Geisenhof
1976 – 1977	Jay Geisenhof
1975 – 1976	Jay Geisenhof

Southside Businessman's Club

Following the merger of Jacksonville and South Jacksonville, in early 1932, the Southside Business Men's Club was founded by a few civic minded men who wanted to improve the working environment of the Southside of Jacksonville. At that time, the Southside's link with

226

Jacksonville was by one bridge and an old ferryboat. Only one telephone existed on the Southside and records show that it was number 367 belonging to a Mrs. H.P. Phillips.

Early leaders of the Southside Business Men's Club recognized the need for banks, major businesses and adequate schools to be built and they set about the task of accomplishing the goals of making this side of the river a safe and prosperous part of Jacksonville.

Evidence of one of the Club's earliest accomplishments is the Southside Branch Library. The library is the result of the Club obtaining an appropriation for its construction. The cornerstone of the library reads – "Through united community effort, this building stands as a constant reminder of the initiative, energy, and devoted service of the Southside Business Men's Club." Another example of their diligence for improvement is Baptist Hospital. The hospital solicited and received the Club's assistance in obtaining its' charter.

Meeting first in the back of the Lane Drug Store at 2011 San Marco Boulevard, where the Bank of America branch now stands, they decided to meet weekly in order to stay abreast of the issues of the day. They next met aboard the old "City of Jacksonville," a retired stern-paddle wheeler tied up where Baptist Medical Center is today. American Legion Post 88 leased the old boat and the ladies Auxiliary charged our members 50 cents for their hot lunch, 10 cents of which went for the payment of dues. They later met at a restaurant at the intersection then known as "Times Square", now overshadowed by part of the Southside's expressway system. During World War II, the Club met in the employees' dining room at Gibbs Shipyards and later at the old Lobster House Restaurant.

While dining each week on Southside's dilapidated, debris-strewn waterfront, the Club set about plans to convert that shoreline into a waterfront park. Legal work and resolutions were used to acquire the land between the bridges and our members served on the Citizens Advisory Committee during all preplanning phases of Friendship Park. In 1965, the park was dedicated and public officials gave our Club the lion's share of the credit.

Streets, roads and traffic planning have long been a priority of the Club. The old East Coast Railway right-of-way from Southside to the beaches was secured by the Club for the construction of Beach Boulevard. The Club also secured U.S. 1 south of Jacksonville as it is today. We had the honor of naming it Philips Highway after Judge Philips and we were in charge of its dedication when Governor Sholtz cut the ribbon to open it on July 12, 1934.

The Club did an outstanding job of fighting for the Main Street Bridge. We were again in charge of the ceremonies in 1940 when governor Holland cut the ribbon to open it. In 1966, the Club dedicated another road we fought for – Interstate 95 – from Atlantic Boulevard to Bowden Road. Governor Hayden Burns made the dedication remarks.

In mid-1982, recognizing the years of work to secure an overpass at University and Philips highway, the Department of Transportation invited the Club to the site at the onset of construction. There, each member present signed his name on the first piling driven into place by Mayor Jake Godbold, who operated the pile driver. At its completion in March of 1983, we met for lunch on top of the overpass for the dedication ceremonies where the Mayor, local and state dignitaries and officers of the Club cut the ribbon opening the overpass to vehicular traffic. Immediately after the ceremony, the decorations and ribbons were hastily pushed aside as the first vehicle to cross the new overpass was an ambulance on an emergency run.

The youth of Jacksonville has also long been of interest to the Southside Business Men's Club. The early days of Landon High School saw the Club help buy band instruments and uniforms for the school band and the Landon Lionettes, a girl's marching unit that became known nationwide. Over the years our members have built many parks, soccer fields and furnished playground equipment throughout Southside.

Many new schools served Southside's growth in the 1950's and 60's and in 1969 our focus shifted to Pop Warner League projects. At that time, the "Little Gator Bowl" game (a name sanctioned by the Gator Bowl Association and given exclusively to us) was established. Each year, we sponsored the top teams participating in the Pop Warner League as they competed in the mighty Gator Bowl facility for the Championship. Game proceeds were used to sponsor our scholarship fund for deserving Pop Warner boys and girls and to help perpetuate Pop Warner activities in Jacksonville. We felt their programs fostered principles of honesty, self-sacrifice and fair play in our youth.

Back in the 1930s, the roster of the Club was limited to a maximum of 30 members, but as South Jacksonville grew, so did our membership. In 1977, under the direction of C. Lee Daniel, club membership grew to an all-time high of 400 members. A motion was presented to the board to limit membership, however, it failed.

In 1993, City Council Resolution 93-132-37 outlined the Club's history and proclaimed to the city of Jacksonville that proper recognition was given to the Club for its years of service to the community. A framed copy of the resolution was presented to a large contingent of past Presidents who gathered in Council Chambers to accept the Resolution on behalf of the Club's entire membership. It was a prestigious honor indeed.

1994 saw the emergence of our Club-created Youth Achievement Program (YAP) masterminded by past presidents Fred Harford and Gene Bushor. This program, together with the schools, recognizes youths who are contributing to their school and its neighborhood, notably through involvement with the school's safety patrol. Once a school is chosen, and after fund-raising by Club members and school faculty and parents, forty percent of the money raised is immediately given directly to the school for use toward an event or activity of their choice. The other sixty percent of the money raised during these events goes into the Club's Charity account for use in providing college scholarships to those same children when they enter college. On May 26, 1998, the City Council honored our Club with reference to our Youth Achiever Program with a Resolution (98-422-A).

In 1995 the Club elected its African-American president, Tyrone Townsend. Tyrone is also credited with creating the "Kids Shopping Spree" in the mid 1980's. Christmas charity work for disadvantaged Southside children has been underway for almost three decades. Scores of children and their families are happier by the actions of this Club during the holiday season. For the first several years K-Mart opened its doors to the Club and the kids. In 2003 the Club initiated a formal relationship with the Target Company's Mandarin store to assist in fulfilling the Christmas dreams of many of Jacksonville area's underprivileged children.

Also In 1995, at the City's request, the Club adopted Treaty Oak Park near the river and planted a splendid rose garden.

In 1996 the membership voted to admit women for the first time. Fittingly, Pauline W. Smith, the Executive Secretary of the Club since 1959, was voted as the Club's first female member as well as the first female lifetime honorary member. She was also elected to a three year term on Board of Governors, making her the first female Board member. Pauline retired in 2000 after 41 years of faithful service. Each year we now recognize a local college student in Pauline's honor with the Pauline W. Smith Scholarship Award.

That same year also saw the birth of the Clubs first Annual Charity Golf Classic, which netted $5,000 for our scholarship program in its' inaugural year. The tireless efforts of past president Crump Kirby and member Jay Cann are directly responsible for many thousands of dollars donated to the Club's charities account from this annual event.

In 1999, the Club established a building fund that will one day allow our Club to have a permanent meeting place.

In 2004, for the first time in the history of the SBMC a woman vice-president presided over a weekly meeting. Belinda Mitchell, then Vice President and Branch Manager for Center Bank of Jacksonville went on to become the first woman to be elected president for the year 2006. One of her favorite accomplishments included the first Club parade float entry in

231

the Veterans Day Parade, resulting in a well-deserved recognition from the Office of the Mayor.

One of the Club's greatest accomplishments was exceeding $100,000.00 in the SBMC Charities Fund, which is used to provide scholarships to eligible students from Jacksonville's Southside. This occurred in 2005 and while that milestone was taking place, we also built a playground for the Children's Home Society. 2005 President, Steve Johnston, established a new award to be given annually, the "Volunteer of the Year" award. The first ever Volunteer of the Year award was given to Art Fields for his willingness to support our Club by volunteering at every Club event.

In 2007 the Southside Business Men's Club, under the leadership of President Tom Harris, proudly celebrated its 75th Anniversary. The year was highlighted by a 75th Anniversary Gala which not only celebrated the club's past but also honored the many achievements of the club's past presidents. That same year began the Clubs efforts to assist the St. John's River Alliance in its' efforts to obtain funding for a State of Florida specialty license plate, and longtime club member Charles McBurney was elected to the Florida House of Representatives.

In 2008 the club had another first. Angelo Volpe, after many years of dedicated work on all programs and activities of the club, became the first Canadian citizen to be president of the Southside Business Men's Club. He initiated work on a much needed, more businesslike look for the new SBMC web site.

The history of this great Club was attained by individuals actively engaged in a vision of the future. We do not intend to rest on their laurels; rather, we seek active involvement from energetic leaders of our Southside business community to add their mark to these hallowed pages. The message is clear – Get Involved!

In 2009 President Tim Buchanan brought the club up to date with a complete overhaul of the By-Laws. Also, Political Action committee started our Annual trip to Tallahassee to meet with State Representatives.

2010 - Gene Maszy was elected President for a second time when President Greg Tucker needed to step down due to a job change. Gene was also President in 2003.

2011 - Ken Dean was our President and the club embarked on a new mission. Our Charities started the VIP (VETERANS INDEPENDENCE PROJECT). This program supports Jacksonville's wounded Veterans returning home from service. The Wounded Warrior Project already helps them with a job and place to live, but they need so much more (household goods) Towels, sheets, pots, pans, pantry items etc. The V I P will help supply these items. After all, Jacksonville is a military town and we love our veterans.

Presidents

2016   Patrick Heatherington
2015   Tim Howe
2014   Annie Howe
2013   Jepp Walter
2012   Galina Schott
2011   Ken Dean
2010   Greg Tucker/Gene Maszy
2009   Tim Buchanan

2008   Angelo Volpe
2007   Tom Harris
2006   Belinda Mitchell
2005   Steve Johnston
2004   Jim Parrish
2003   Gene R. Maszy
2002   Win Thomas
2001   Tom Carroll
2000   John M. Hamel
1999   Crump Kirby
1998   Fred S. Harford, Jr.
1997   Randy Scott
1996   Mark Wilkinson
1995   Tyrone P. Townsend
1994   Eugene L. Bushor
1993   Richard W. Campbell*
1992   Thomas R. Sikes
1991   Brian E. Bock
1990   John J. Kelly, Jr.*
1989   Frank H. Stone
1988   John Martin
1987   David L. Young
1986   Robert S. Cooper*
1985   William W. O'Nale, Jr.
1984   Bud Shutterly
1983   Ken Williams
1982   Robert L. Cox*
1981   Robert A. Sabourin
1980   Larry Flynn
1979   William P. Tuggle, Jr.*
1978   Earl W. Jorgensen
1977   C. Lee Daniel, Jr.*
1976   Paul J. Shields*
1975   Allan G. Gimbel

1974   A. J. Pionessa*
1973   Alvin M. Towns, Sr.*
1972   Dole J. Kelley, Jr.*
1971   T. Marvin Duncan*
1970   Jimmie W. Harden
1969   Forrest G. Ashmead*
1968   Sherley R. Dunn*
1967   James T. Tresca
1966   Sam I. Smith, Jr.
1965   R. John Crider
1964   Gifford Grange, Jr.
1963   A. D. Smith*
1962   James C. Harper
1961   James C. Harper
1960   Carl A. Chambliss*
1959   W.A. Weatherford*
1958   John C. Coleman*
1957   Stuart Edwards*
1956   C. Donald MacLean, Jr.
1955   R. M. Naugle*
1954   V. Thomas Early*
1953   L. E. Hakes*
1952   Donald A. Bolton*
1951   Olin F. Wolfe*
1950   Carl V. Cesery*
1949   Carl V. Cesery*
1948   George W. Martin*
1947   George W. Martin*
1946   Maynard C. Burrell*
1945   Harry A. Pierce*
1944   Harry A. Pierce*
1943   W. Rufus Thompson*
1942   Russell R. Moore*
1941   Russell R. Moore*

1940   Norman C. Edwards*
1939   Norman C. Edwards*
1932-1938   Carl M. Taylor*
*deceased

Source: Crump Kirby, www.southsidebusinessmensclub.com

Artists, Athletes, Writers and More...

Elmer Apple, Jr. – Basketball – Jacksonville Junior College Green Dolphins.

Keenan Bell – Baseball – University of Florida.

Tyrie A. Boyer – Writer – *Memories and Reflections of a Florida Cracker* (2012).

Soren Brockdorf – Writer - *Of One Blood* (2009).

E. Zimmermann Boulos –
International Soccer Referee for FIFA
1996 Olympic Qualification Tournament
Preliminary rounds 1994 World Cup
Preliminary rounds 1998 World Cup
1996 Major League Soccer
1997 Major League Soccer
1983 NCAA Men's Division 1 Championship

Brittany Bowald – Track – Jacksonville University.

Robert Broward – Writer/Architect – Georgia Tech.
Books: *The Broward Family: From France to Florida, The Architecture of Henry John Klutho The Prairie School in Jacksonville* (1st ed. 1983, 2nd rev. ed. 2003).

Janaya Chambers – Track – University of Georgia.

Clio Chazan-Gabbard – Ballet – Danced role of Clara in the Florida Ballet Nutcracker.

Andy Cheney – Basketball – University of Florida.

Ted Copeland – Basketball – University of Florida.

Storm Davis – Major League Baseball – Baltimore Orioles (1982–1986), San Diego Padres (1987), Oakland Athletics (1987–1989), Kansas City Royals (1990–1991), Baltimore Orioles (1992), Oakland Athletics (1993), Detroit Tigers (1993–1994).

Brian DiLoreto – Soccer - University of Tampa.

E. Lanier Drew – Swimming, Basketball, Cross-country – Trinity College - Hartford. 1984 and 1988 Olympic Trials Marathon.

Hugh Durham – Basketball – Florida State University. Coach: Florida State University, University of Georgia, Jacksonville University. Inducted into the National Collegiate Basketball Hall of Fame in 2016.

Dave Engdahl – Architect, Sculptor.

C.J. Fluharty – Musician.

Hannah Fluharty – Soccer – Francis Marion University.

George Foote – Baseball – Methodist University, Off-ice Official (penalty box) with East Coast Hockey League. Books: *Hendricks Haiku Project* (2009), *Hendricks Haiku Project II* (2014).

Regan Foote – Fencing – University of Florida.

238

Teddy Foster – Baseball – University of Florida.

John Gooding – Marching Band – University of Florida.

Ashley Halil – Writer – Books: *Comin' Across Grace* (2013), *The Sleepless Knight* (2015), *King's Daze* (2016).

John Harmeling – Football – Florida State University.

Addie Higgins – Ballet – Danced the role of Clara in the First Coast Nutcracker.

Andy Hogshead – Crew – Harvard University.

Nancy Hogshead – Swimming – Duke University. 1984 Olympics - Gold Medals in the 100m freestyle, 4x100m freestyle relay, 4x100 medley relay. Silver Medal in the 200m individual medley.

Sally Bartel Hogshead – Writer and Speaker – Duke University. Books: *Radical Careering* (2005), *Fascinate* (2010), *How the World Sees You* (2014) *Fascinate: How to make your brand impossible to resist* (2016) NYT Best Seller List three times, #1 IBD.

Tanner Lane – Theater & Dance – Florida State University. Currently, a lead dancer/singer in the Radio City Music Hall Christmas Spectacular.

Marty LaPrade – Football – Furman University.

Lianne Mananquil – Soccer – Rice University.

Charles Martin – Writer – Florida State University. Books: *Long Way Gone* (2016), *Water from My Heart* (2016), *A Life Intercepted* (2015), *River Road* (2015), *Unwritten* (2013), *Thunder and Rain* (2012), *The Mountain Between Us* (2010), *Where the River Ends* (2008*), Chasing Fireflies: A Novel of Discovery* (2007), *Maggie* (2006), *When Crickets Cry* (2006), *Wrapped in Rain* (2005) and *The Dead Don't Dance* (2004).

Mandy McGlynn –Soccer – Virginia Tech. Member of the U18 Team USA.

Eileen Shannon Moore – Painter.

Joanelle Mulrain – Painter.

Scott Norton – Distance runner – Jacksonville University.

Charles E. Patillo III – Writer, *St. Dunstan's and John.*

Hadley Parrish-Cotton – Singer/Songwriter/Guitarist – Reed College.

Al Poindexter – Singer/Songwriter/Banjo player extrodinaire.

Herbert Hill Peyton – Writer – *Newboy.*

Sid Roberson – Baseball – University of North Florida. Drafted by the Milwaukee Brewers in the 29th round of the draft in 1992. Spent the summer of 1992 playing on Team USA. Made it to the major leagues with the Milwaukee Brewers in 1995. #73 on Times Union list of 100 best athletes of the Century.

Robin Robinson - Writer, *Southbank Sojourn: A Photographic Journey Through The Early Days of San Marco and South Jacksonville (Jacksonville Preservation Award)*

Debra Webb Rogers – Writer/Dancer – Books: *Dancing in Time,* (EPIC Award Finalist), *San Marco, Jacksonville's Southside* (Jacksonville Preservation Award), and a Christmas short story, *One Single Present* (First Place Award, JournEzine.com). A former professional ballet dancer who performed with The Birmingham Ballet, The Florida Ballet and The Israel Ballet.

Ginny Stine Romano - Architecture School of Design, University of Florida. Fine Artist {oil painting}, Textile & Jewelry Designer.

Shaun Salari – Baseball – Erskine College.

Traci Salari – Best Elementary School Teacher (Folio Magazine, 2010), Author (*Trusting and Supporting Teachers*, International Literary Association).

Ernie Saltmarsh – Football – Florida State University.

Karen Saltmarsh – Writer – *This Tree Has a Story.*

Suzanne Saltmarsh – Dancer/Choreographer/Writer – BFA Florida State University, MFA Jacksonville University. Studied with Marta Jackson School of dance and the Florida Ballet. Artistic director of Saltmarsh Dance of Jacksonville. Performed with Martha Graham Dance Company, San Francisco Opera Ballet, Dallas Black Dance Theater Toward and performed at Kennedy Center, Queen Elizabeth US Tour 1992. Choreographer for Marin Ballet, San Francisco SOTA,

Booker T. Washington SOTA, Douglas Anderson SOTA, Florida Ballet, Dallas Black Dance Theatre, FSU dance dept.

Garrett Scantling – Decathlete, University of Georgia, 3 time SEC champion, First alternate 2106 Olympic Team.

Hunter Scantling – Baseball, Florida State University & Detroit Tigers Farm System.

Michael Scantling – Football, Valdosta State University.

Jacob Skiles – Pianist, University of Alabama Birmingham.

Chris Soha – Collegiate Martial Arts, UCF, 2nd degree blackbelt.

George Soha – Football – Massachusetts Marine Academy.

Joseph Soha – Wrestling – Massachusetts Marine Academy.

Mike Soha III – Weightlifter – LSU Shreveport. Number one in the nation in his weight group for 2 years.

Jennifer Stehlin – Cheerleader – University of Florida.

Roger Strickland – Basketball – 1963, First round pick, Los Angeles Lakers.

Jackie Sullivan – Dance/Theatre – University of South Florida.

Jeannie Szaltis – Watercolorist, artist, and instructor.

Robert R. Tebow, II – Fellowship of Christian Athletes – NE Florida Rep., University of Florida.

Dale Tedder – Writer – Foundations for Godly Manhood (2016).

Clara Trednick – Ballet – Philadelphia Rock School of Dance.

Jeff Trippe – Writer/Musician – University of Florida. Books: *Onward to Planet Copius: Through Time and Space* (2015), *The Pride of the Panthers* (2014), *Far From My Own Shore* (2015), *This Brittle Existence* (2007), *Lawsuits of the Rich and Famous* (1994).

Philip Trippe – Ice Hockey – Appalachian State University.

Connor Vaughan – Distance runner – University of Florida.

Cynthia Walburn – Artist – Transcendent Impressionism, BA/MA University of Florida.

Sheri Webber – Editor & Writer – Original titles: *Dawn Rising*; *The Prodigy Series*; *Plainly Said*; *Madstone*; *Love Again, Die Again*; *Letters from Uganda*; *Freak Field*; and *Devil Went Down*.

Judy Wells – Travel writer/photographer.

Mark Woods – Writer – *Lassoing the Sun.*

Martin Zubero – Swimmer – University of Florida. Olympic Gold Medalist – 200m backstroke.

Bishop Kenny Baseball players drafted into MLB:

1970's
Brad Hoch, 1971, Indians - Pat McMahon, 1971, Mets
Greg Charleston, 1971, Mets

1980's
Joel Chavous, 1982, Phillies - Tommy Raffo, 1986, Orioles
Charlie Anderson, 1988, Cardinals - Todd Dunn, 1989,
Brewers

1990's
Drew Williams, 1990, Brewers - Brian Wilkes, 1993, Indians
Kevin Witt, 1994, Blue Jays - Travis Chapman, 1996, Phillies
John Edward Raffo, 1996, Mets - Derek Rix, 1996, Red Sox
Matt Schneider, 1996, Pirates - Daniel Hodges, 1999, Phillies
Jonathan Papelbon, 1999, Red Sox

2000's
Tony Richie, 2000, Cubs - Darren O'Day, 2001, Angels
A. J. Johnson, 2002, Cubs - Jeremy Papelbon, 2002, Cubs
Mat Gamel, 2003, Brewers - Jeff Flagg, 2004, Mets
Daniel Schuh, 2005, Nationals - Joey Bergman, 2006,
Cardinals - Jimmy Howick, 2008, Astros

2010's
Ben Gamel, 2010, Yankees

River Run – Top finishers from the 32207 zip code.

Year – Male – Female

2016 – Conner Vaughn – Tracey Kuhn
2015 – Neil Chandler – Tracey Kuhn
2014 – Christopher McCaffrey – Tracey Kuhn
2013 – Jason Graham – Erin Dankworth
2012 – Chris Gruwell – Jamie Shelton
2011 – Chris Gruwell – JC Pinto

Source: Stuart Toomey, 1st Place Sports

Hendricks Avenue Baseball 10U Allstars*
District Championship Team 2016

Coaches: Jay Kaplan and Erik Pietschker
Players:

Name	Positions
Ben Oberdorfer	1B, C
Bryson Harnage	P, 2B
Camden Harnage	RF, 1B
Isaac DeCastro	OF, 2B
Land Johnson	3B
Levi Pietchker	P, CF
Luke Sheffield	3B, C
Maddox Fox	P, 3B
Matthew Sanchez	2B, 3B
Sam Kaplan	P, LF, 3B
Tommy Brice	P, SS
William Rosenberg	P, INF

*Source: HendricksBaseball.org

Hendricks Avenue Elementary Chess –
Hendricks Avenue Elementary won their first Jacksonville Scholastic Chess Championship in 1997.

1996-1997 City Championship Team:

Taylor Blackburn, Beau Cheatwood, Madison Cheatwood, Garrett Foote, Joseph Foote, Max Higgs, Chris McCaffrey, Michael McCaffrey, Joseph Meek, Jessica Roberts, Stuart Smith, Aaron Stephens, and Joanna Truett.

In all, the Hendricks Avenue Elementary Chess Team has now won 12 City Championships since earning that first crown in 1997.

Coming full circle, here is the roster of the Hendricks players that won the 2016 City Championship;

K-2 Division: David Booher, Madi Bowyer, James Brandler, Romeo Cannata, Charlie DeVooght, Gabriel Merchan, Jeb Naugle, Julian Norris, Lucy Pearson, Josh Postal, Lucas Repper, Avisa Rezaei, Jude Yu.

3-5 Division: Charlie Alesandro, Hayes Bettman, Thomas Brandler, Katherine Cheshire, James Francis, Quinn Gray, David Jenson, Gabriel Keiter, Noah Lunsberry, Keegan MacLean, Emiliano Makros, Corey Menard, Jack O'Malley, Parker Phan, Elias Piquer, Niek Rezaei, Parker Roberson, Sean Thompson, and Esher Yu.

Feast of Carnevale
Anita Morrill – Empty Nest Boutique Events

On Sunday, November 6th, 2016, The San Marco Merchants Association was thrilled to celebrate *San Marco's 90th Birthday: Feast of Carnevale*. Over 150 guests delighted their senses at a banquet-style feast in Balis Park, the heart of San Marco Square, while reveling in the rich history and raising a glass to 90 years of community. To mark this milestone occasion, banquet fare was prepared by the acclaimed chefs of *The San Marco Dining District*; Chef Matthew Medure (Matthew's), Chef Sam Efron (Taverna), Chef Tom Gray (Town Hall/Moxie), Chef Wesley Nogueira (bb's Restaurant) and Chef Chris Cohen (Bistro Aix).

The origins of the celebration's Venetian theme hearken back to the beginnings of the San Marco neighborhood that all Jacksonville loves today. Over ninety years ago, San Marco was constructed on 80-plus acres of the former Villa Alexandria estate in what was then known as South Jacksonville. Developer Telfair Stockton imagined the area as a fashionable, upscale development comprised of 250 lots and a centralized commercial district. Construction of the first buildings began in 1926 and was planned in the Italian Renaissance revival style, influencing the final name of the community and its streets. San Marco Square, named after Venice's Piazza San Marco, showcases several Mediterranean-style buildings and a central fountain guarded by three regal lions, a symbol of St. Mark.

The Venetian-styled bash featured live music, masked Carnevale revelers, a stilt walker, performances by Jacksonville Dance Theatre, and a closing toast by local opera singer Regina Torres.

Party Revelers *(note: some guests may not be listed)*

Geddes & Marla Anderson
Tracy Arthur
Desiree Bailey
Mike and Gail Balanky
Janis Bebeau & Connie Smith
E Zimmermann & Terri Boulos
Jimmy & Benita Boyd
Lori & Tyrie Boyer
Michele & Paul Boynton
Forrest Brewer & Ward Lariscy
Bronie & Joash Brunet
Dee Burke
Karina Cadora
Joseph & Victoria Carlucci
Karen & Matt Carlucci
Lauren & Matt Carlucci, Jr.
Michael Carlucci
James & Rula Carr
Joni & Tommy Clark
Edmund Clark
Cyndy Clayton
Linda Cliff
Alan & Ellen Cotrill
Alice Coughlin
Leanna & Hussein Cumber
Jeff & Susan Curry
Joel David
Brian Ware
Terry & John Donovan
Alex E.
Kiley Efron
Eddie Fink & Dawn Ladd
Kenneth Flottman

Steve & Deanna Furey
Julie Gaines
Ivan & Jennifer Gordon
Catherine & David Graham
Robert & Paola Harris
Dale Harris & Phyllis Rice
Gwen & Alan Howard
Sara Marie Johnston
Nan Kavanaugh & Scottie Schwartz
Bill & Tracy Langley
Wendy & Marty LaPrade
Lisa & Scott Leuthold
Betsy Lovett
Tim & Diane Martin
Susan Masucci & Katie McCaughan
Nate Mayo
Karen & Buddy McCombs
Alice McCoy
Chris & Barbara McMorrow
Alex Mejias
Julio Cesar Mendez
Antoinette & Louis Merchan
Adam & Dana Merrill
David & Monique Miller
Anita Morrill
Joanelle Mulrain
Kathleen & Seth Pajcic
Suzanne Perritt
Lindey & Ryan Riggs
Jude & Heidi Roberts
Jay & Robin Robinson
Peter & Lee Ann Rummell
Devon & Lauren Scheible
Ellen Setzer
Patti Stanford

Dinner Revelers Enjoying "The Feast"

Venetian Strollers

Karen & Matt Carlucci

Betsey Lovett & Ward Lariscy

Forrest Brewer & Betsey Lovett

Robert & Paola Harris & Guests
252

Leanna Cumber, Councilwoman Lori Boyer & Tyrie Boyer

Pete & Anita Vining & Guests

Feast of Carnevale "Revelers"

Joel David & Brian Ware

Anita & Pete Vining

Ari Gaskin, Lauren Alderman & Daniel Austin

Jeannie Smith & Patti Stanford

Paola & Robert Harris

Steve & Deanna Furey & Eddie Fink
257

Paul & Shelly Boynton

Barbara & Chris McMorrow

Sarah Marie Johnston, Desiree Bailey, Kiley Efron
& Nan Kavanaugh

Anita Morrill/Event Planner-Empty Nest Boutique Events

Chef Sam Efron - Taverna & Chris Cohen - Bistro Aix

Chef Tom Gray - Town Hall/Moxie Kitchen + Cocktails,
Chef Wesley Nogueira - bb's, and Chefs Alexander Yim and
Matthew Medure - Matthew's